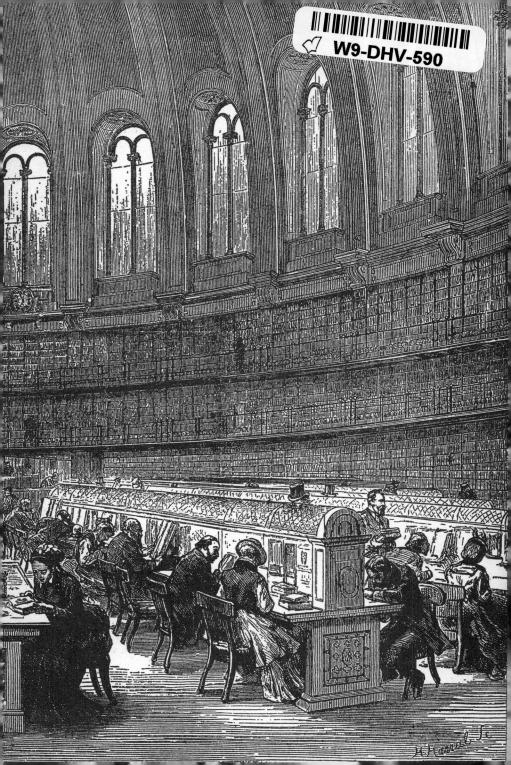

William B. Bjornstad
June 10, 1952

BY FRANK SWINNERTON

A London Bookman

THE BOOKMAN'S
LONDON

By
FRANK SWINNERTON

1952
DOUBLEDAY & COMPANY, INC.
GARDEN CITY, NEW YORK

Library of Congress Catalog Card Number 52–6362

First published, 1952, in the United States

Contents

List of Plates

Note

I hope this book will be found interesting and amusing. It has been written at the suggestion of the publishers, who must bear responsibility for the fact that it is personal and discursive; every other fault arises from my own shortcomings. I have an unrequited passion for facts, and have inserted a great many of these from my own knowledge and memory; but I should feel dishonest if I did not say here that I have found incalculable support in the great Wheatley book, *London, Past and Present*, and Mr Frank Mumby's *Publishing and Bookselling*. Mr Fred Urquhart very kindly sent me some valuable tips for the last chapter; among others from whom I have borrowed, Mrs Thirkell kindly permits the extract from *Three Houses* and Mr C. D. Medley three quotations from *George Moore*; and I wish to thank two true friends, Mr Vernon Rendall and Mr S. K. Ratcliffe, for reading through the typescript or proofs. Neither of these helpers should be blamed for my incapacities. I think this is all I need say, except that the book was written with the knowledge that it was to be well illustrated, and that the illustrations have been chosen by Mr Charles Fry, who in this work received extraordinarily valuable help from Messrs W. T. Spencer of New Oxford Street.

F.S.

I

The London Scene

1 *London; the London of Dickens; Clerkenwell; Farringdon Road bookstalls*

If you were to ask representative Londoners their views of London, you would receive a strange medley of answers; and few of them would be free from arrogance. One such answer—it is probably the best of all—would quote Dr Johnson's remark that the man who is tired of London is tired of life. If not the best, it is a good answer, because it emphasises the inexhaustible interest of a city in which age, busyness, government, courage, architectural irregularity, wealth, smoke, and good humour jumble together the history and characteristics of a whole people.

Another answer, in which pride is naked, would echo the reply of a cockney who, when asked by a Canadian recruiting officer if he meant that he was born in London, Ontario, scornfully retorted "Naow! London the 'ole bloody world!"

Yet another would stress the extraordinary anonymity of its citizens, who, besides respecting the privacy of their neighbours, carry the foible of incuriousness and non-acquaintance to excess, and often do not know the names of those who live on each side of them unless by rare error a letter is misdelivered. In such cases the letter is handed back to another postman. "We don't ashoshiate," said the ground-floor lady to my mother, when we lived on the first floor of a slum house: it was really a compliment that she should speak at all, and her explanation of previous and subsequent aloofness was gravely accepted as truth by one who had come in childhood from the North.

I should warn you, however, that most of the answers you received to your question would probably be improvised. The Londoner, shrewd, caustic, irreverent, but—I repeat—essentially good-humoured, has always added to his incuriousness a denial of responsibility for the grandeur of his home. He is detached. He has never gone sightseeing. Lamb apart, all students and encomiasts of London, from Dr Johnson to James Bone, have come to town from far away.

As a Londoner by birth and long residence, I have been trying, in order to set this book against a background of the London scene, to

1

recover every memory of what I first knew of that scene. And, do what I will, I cannot escape from an atmosphere of autumn, of dusk, overwhelming skies, mud-fringed setts, alley-ways, narrow streets, and, oddly enough, small hills as well as incalculable twists. There is something important about those hills, whether they fall from Fleet Street or the Strand, from Dover Street, Ludgate Hill (a giant among lesser descents), Piccadilly, Holborn, or Farringdon Road. There is also perpetuated history in the ancient courts and alley-ways, as Dickens well knew. As for the season of the year, autumnal dusk is the most beautiful light of all in which to see and relish the London I remember.

Dickens knew everything there was to know about the atmosphere of London. He loved the streets, whether they were cold and dry, or cold and slushy, as long as they were crowded, as they usually are. He loved the sight of the poulterers' and butchers' shops as they were in his day (and in mine, as a child), and the grocers' festooned windows, and the parcels and bottles of Christmas, and even the staggering gait of homegoers who had too bumperously greeted the Children's Feast. He loved to walk the streets at night, surrounded by grotesques, feeling their human nature common with his own, seeing all oddities and treasuring them; seeing, also, the drawn faces, the evil faces, and the jovial faces, and reading behind them the stories of their owners' lives. An alley-way, for him, spelt romance. Not romance sweetened with sugar, but romance in the sense of life spiced and coloured with every bizarre possibility. Do you remember Scrooge's dwelling-place? It was "a gloomy suite of rooms, in a lowering pile of building up a yard, where it had so little business to be, that one could scarcely help fancying it must have run there when it was a young house, playing at hide-and-seek with other houses, and forgotten the way out again."

I think that is extraordinarily suggestive. Certainly it is suggestive of the London I knew as a child, in the days of gas-lamps and exquisite shadows, of fogs, silent passers, the jingle of bells upon horse-drawn tram-cars, the desperately thrilling shout—"Hiee-hiee-hiee"—of the firemen as their engines were galloped along, and the tempting, frightening darkness of unexpected openings among the houses, through which one saw stone flags, iron railings, dim houses, and the unknown. Those who write scornfully of Dickens as a melodramatic writer have not lived, as I did, in the London of Dickens.

I agree that my London is not an immense territory. It stretches a finger farthest towards the north of the town, where I was born and where, for a time, my home was. It does not extend beyond Bishops-gate and Fenchurch Street in the east nor Hammersmith or Notting Hill in the west. When I have crossed the Thames bridges I am soon, though not immediately, in a strange land. But, after years of diminish-ing familiarity, I am still as much at home in that small central heart of London as I was fifty and sixty years ago. I find my way unerringly on foot; in a taxi I half-unconsciously judge the driver's knowledge and skill by the route he takes. One learns a town in childhood, as one learns a language or a poem, so that it cannot be forgotten.

In London, the never-ending, one dare not dream of knowing the whole. One must be content with a district, or districts. And although I was not born, as is sometimes said in print, in Clerkenwell, I lived there until I was eight years old, not five minutes' walk from "Gwynne Place, formerly Granville Place," which is better known to the world today as Riceyman Steps. When I first read Arnold Bennett's book I said to myself: "It isn't Clerkenwell; he doesn't *know* it as he knows the Five Towns." You see I thought I *knew* it. Was that merely vanity?

My grandfather's house, a tall, plain residence in a row of such houses, was at the highest point of Farringdon Road, from which the road descends upon one side towards King's Cross (it becomes Union Road within a few yards), while on the other it goes south towards Blackfriars. Though some of its neighbours were less lucky, this house escaped Hitler's bombs, and continues to face, not, as in my day, the wall of a prison, but the milder dreariness of Mount Pleasant Parcels Post Office. There is still a Mount Pleasant here; but its greater day was before the making of Rosebery Avenue, which I remember. And when, as a choirboy in the now bomb-wrecked church of St Mary, Aldermanbury, I walked with my brother, in 1890 or there-abouts, to attend the services, it was from number 150 Farringdon Road that we set out.

We went downhill to Farringdon Street, took an upward turn through Smithfield, and then along Cheapside to the City; and there was something unearthly in the sound of church-bells challenging one another above the absolutely silent streets. I need not say that there were no bookstalls in Farringdon Road at any hour on Sundays. Nor were there any cattle in Smithfield Market, although on weekdays I often awakened in darkness to hear the whispering shuffle of sheep as they passed our home; and, as I recollect it, no horse omnibuses or carts or hansom cabs were to be seen at that hour of the evening. All was open to the eye, and might have formed part of a deserted town.

The bookstalls were busy enough on weekdays; for even then they were as much of an institution as the quayside stalls of Paris. They did not enjoy the poetic fame of the Parisian stalls, which have space, atmosphere, and publicised romance. They were closely crowded, as they are today, with much irrelevant junk; and to juvenile eyes were no more than a tatterdemalion market of the unwanted. One needed to be an enthusiast to face books supercoated with London dirt, which I never did, or perhaps was never encouraged to do. But these stalls represented the least pretentious of all appeals to bibliomania. They were the poor man's browsing ground. I like to believe that my father spent pennies and twopences at them for his curious little library—Burns, Pope, the Arabian Nights, Dickens, Emerson, Carlyle, and the rest—in days before W. T. Stead flooded us with those badly-printed orange-covered booklets, the Penny Poets, their pale blue consorts, the sometimes abridged Penny Novelists, and the pink Books for the Bairns. If he did not do so, at least he gave me the first chance of seeing one of the most respectable passions of men at work, the passion for the printed page.

2 Paternoster Row; Fleet Street; Death of Queen Victoria

It is London's connection with the printed page, and those who deal in the printed page and its contents, that is the subject of this book; so it will be fitting if I say here that in those days the wealthier buyers of secondhand books spent most of their shillings and half-crowns in Paternoster Row or Holywell Street. When I was fourteen, and a newspaper office boy, I saw them doing it. It was a part of my work to deliver voucher copies of some weekly journals to publishers and advertising agents who did not want them; and I had constantly to trudge the length of the Row and at least some portion of Holywell Street with my papers. I loitered in both thoroughfares, ignorant of the bad reputation of the second (it was a reputation merely for the kind of books—Maria Monk, paper-covered Decamerons, Heptamerons, and so on—to be found there), but already relishing the narrow, gloomy splendours of the first, which you may think I exaggerate.

They were, or so I feel, great splendours. They had been, although (having at that time not read Stow's *Survey of London*) I did

Old Paternoster Row

Farringdon Road, to-day and yesterday

not know it, splendours since the days of Queen Elizabeth. Stow said:

> "This street is now called Paternoster Row because of stationers or text writers that dwelt there, who wrote and sold all sorts of books then in use, A B C with the Pater noster, Ave, Creed, Graces, etc."

It is a present delight to recall this description; but in those days I had a more restricted acquaintance with history than I have now; and I saw Paternoster Row as a place of what may be called contemporary importance. That is what it was. Publishing, you must remember, was largely conducted at the end of last century east of Charing Cross. Not universally, of course, for John Murray, Macmillan, Chapman and Hall, Bentley, Chatto and Windus, Smith, Elder, and others were in the West End; but in such a degree that one said "Paternoster Row" as if it were the home of books, as if Dr Johnson had spent his days and nights there, or as if Scott, Macaulay, Froude, or Henry Thomas Buckle might at any moment step out of the doorways one was about to enter. As for secondhand books, they were to be found in every cranny between the majestic black buildings, with, I recall, big sheets of packing paper hanging up to announce in scrawly chalked capitals the special bargains and discounts to be enjoyed that day.

The buildings towered overhead; the book-fanciers crowded a small and penniless boy into the littered gutters; one burst, it seemed, into a sunlit world upon reaching the open space, where culture ended, between the General Post Office and Cheapside. However odd a countenance it might wear, culture had been glimpsed. It was an odd countenance because Paternoster Row, remote from wheeled traffic, or perhaps remote only from stylish equipages, was engrossed in a single subject; the subject, not really of culture, nor of literature, but of books as manufactured, saleable articles. Please to remember this distinction. It is what an old employer of mine used to call "crucial." We shall hear more of it later.

You could step nearer to the Bank and find at least one of the best shops in the kingdom where new books only were sold. You could find lesser shops on Ludgate Hill and in Fleet Street and the Strand. I knew them all. I did not enter them. I stared in their windows. Fleet Street, in particular, was for me as romantic as the Indies. Fleet Street and its picturesque figures.

The office in which I worked was on the second floor of a building half way down Bouverie Street. On the floor below was established for a time a new penny weekly review, edited by a tall young man with a long, thin, fair moustache. He wore a frock coat and a top hat; and his name was Harold Gorst. His father, Sir John Gorst, was a well known Member of Parliament; but it is Harold Gorst I remember, partly because it was in his paper, which was called *The Review of the Week*, that words of mine, in the form of a letter to the Editor, first appeared in print. I was fourteen. He was the first journalist who, for me, ever wore a halo.

I wanted to be a journalist. I thought all the men I saw in Fleet Street were journalists. Alas, the only two whose journalism I ever verified were Clement Shorter, a swarthy, plump man with a cluster of glossy curls under the back brim of his hat and a bundle of review copies of new books under his arm, and Ernest Parke, editor of *The Morning Leader*, also bushy-haired, and wearing a wide-brimmed Quakerish hat. I saw both in the late afternoons; dreaming then of my own future journalistic feats, which have never been performed.

It must have been always fine in those days—eighteen ninety-nine and thereabouts;—for my memory of Fleet Street is either of dusk or of hot summer days. Every so often, as if a lid had been raised, and a galaxy of noisy imps released, dozens of ragged boys and men, in speckled rubber shoes, would come flying from the side streets, hoarsely shouting "Winner!" I cannot remember that the song ever had any other burden, except murder; there were no losers. But the newly-printed contents bills those boys sometimes unfurled as they ran would discreetly announce "Oval Centuries" or "Sussex Collapse." Men caught the papers and pressed ha'pennies into the newsboys' hands. Papers were a ha'penny then, and worth the money.

The men wore boaters and starched collars; some of them, like Harold Gorst, top hats. They wore, as he did, moustaches. My impression is that a good many of them looked like the photographs of Dr Crippen. They filled the pavements, and dawdled more than men now do in Fleet Street. Somehow there was more time. The omnibuses plying up and down the Street were all slowly horse-drawn. They were usually dark green—I remember some of them bore the word "Favorite" in big letters on their sides;—but some, here or elsewhere, were of a beautiful creamy white. At Ludgate Circus the conductors all bawled a mystic word which sounded like "Cobbolstreeterbenk." They meant to say "Liverpool Street and Bank."

As I said, all the omnibuses were horse-drawn. All carts, vans, and lorries, even those bearing huge rolls of what is now called newsprint, but what used to be called paper, were drawn by horses; and one of my earliest admirations was for the skill and courage of the belted boys in dark blue, with glossy-peaked caps, who darted, stooping, right under the horses' noses, brushing dung from the roadway into their dustpan-like shovels and dashing, still doubled up, back to bins at the kerbside.

The offices of an illustrated weekly called *Black and White* were at the top of Bouverie Street, the windows full of photographs and representations of, first, the chief figures and scenes in the Dreyfus trial at Rennes, and then of the Boer War—soldiers crossing rivers, General Buller, "Fighting Mac," and other commanders; President Kruger and his bearded Boer friends; and, of course, the defenders of Ladysmith and Mafeking. Always previously, I suppose, war-pictures had been drawn in line and wash; such drawings, even then, were not quite superseded; but the photographer had arrived.

We had the moving picture ; the flicks—that word was more appropriate then than now, as the movement was really caused by the flicking of successive pages. They had a great vogue, in an open shop near Ludgate Circus. The queues were all for a sort of early strip-tease picture, "Why Marie Blew Out the Light." I never saw this triumph of the Mutoscope. I was too young, and I had no spare pennies; but—like *Photo Bits*—it was a feature of the age.

And, lastly, there were the hawkers' barrows. I do not know if they were moved on as strictly as they are today; but the fresh fruit they sold, the cherries, plums, "fine large strawberries," and some extraordinary, almost crimson tomatoes such as one never sees now, were so cheap that office boys very much like myself would turn away by the score, carrying paper bags, and casually, triumphantly, spitting out cherry stones as they walked off.

Such is my memory of Fleet Street in the nineties—sunshine, dusk, horse omnibuses, Dreyfus and war photographs in the windows, street-sweepers, fruit on the barrows, a strolling, rather shabby crowd, and a shabby, dusty street, with occasional red and white sunblinds, and St Paul's presiding over all. Very hot, with bursts of shouting from the rushing newsboys—always about sport until they cried "Ree-lief-er-Mafeking" or—but I heard that cry, later, in Bedford Street, Covent Garden, one silent evening in nineteen hundred and one—"Death *of* the Queen! Death *of* the Queen!"

3 *The Turn of the Century*

Publishers—and I—were steadily moving west. I ceased for a good many years to enter offices in Fleet Street. There was a new firm, named Methuen, in Essex Street, where the Strand widens to embrace St Clement Danes. It was founded by Mr Algernon Methuen Stedman, who changed his name except upon the title-pages of the school-books he edited, and who in the first years of the twentieth century quite dominated the market in romantic fiction. Other firms, notably that of Fisher Unwin, had gone to the Adelphi, overlooking the Thames. But the streets around Covent Garden were the newest centre of publishing, in spite of the fact that in very recent times Macmillan had moved from Bedford Street to a splendid new building near Leicester Square.

Dent, having taken over Macmillan's old premises, had established the Temple Shakespeare and the Temple Classics; Bliss, Sands and Co. were next door, across the entrance to St Paul's Church; Heinemann, nearly opposite, had just killed the three-volume novel. At the east end of Henrietta Street, round the corner, that bold new venturer Grant Richards (who had come from the big wholesale booksellers, Simpkin, Marshall, in Paternoster Row) had set up his business not far from Duckworth, for whom Edward Garnett was "reading." Farther west along the street was the noble firm of Chapman and Hall, publishers of Dickens and Carlyle, and employers formerly of another famous "reader," George Meredith. Skeffingtons were in King Street; Bells were still in York Street, where they had succeeded Henry G. Bohn; Isbisters in Tavistock Street; and Sands, who published books by "Pitcher," of *The Pink 'Un*, round the corner in Burleigh Street. It was to this world of Covent Garden that I went when I was sixteen.

There has been another shift since those days; and much publishing is now done in Bloomsbury, ideal site for a trade properly radiating from such a symbol of learning and the printed book as the British Museum. But while I grant this, and have friends in Bloomsbury, I feel tenderly towards that fashion of fifty years ago, and I am glad that Covent Garden continues to hold so many publishers. I hope it will always do so.

There, at the beginning of the century, I saw real authors, celebrated authors, for the first time. I sat in a little box in a large showroom, and a brown wire blind across the window of the showroom did little to hide from youthful eyes all who passed up and down Bedford Street. Some carried enormous portfolios; they were recognisably the book-illustrators, or would-be book illustrators, of whom there were too many. Some carried nothing in their hands, but all wisdom in their heads. A number came into my showroom, and it was my business to interview them, which was generally very pleasant; many crossed the street to Heinemann's or Putnam's, the former in particular being magnetic to authors.

One of these authors, I recall, was Hall Caine, who wore such a large black cloak, and such a wide-brimmed black hat, that I thought of him as a wonderful black moth, and imagined his publisher cowering before the gaze of those luminous and protuberant eyes. They were very strange eyes indeed; and as Hall Caine was very lean, and walked with very lithe movements, he was a noticeable figure anywhere. All the same, eyes apart, my own visitors were not less distinguished than he; or so I thought.

In this quiet street, where in spring the door, which had a ball-catch, swung idly to and fro in the breeze, there stood a rank of hansom cabs, around which pigeons and sparrows constantly strutted or busily hopped, picking up the grain which had fallen from the horses' nose-bags. St Paul's Church chimed all the hours. Members of the Yorick Club overhead grew merry as the day advanced. John Martin Harvey —the best Hamlet I ever saw—once ran lightly on the tips of his toes past the cab rank, while several derisive cabbies whistled in time to his buoyant steps. Gilbert Chesterton drove up in other hansoms, which swayed over the pavement as he got out of them. W. H. Hudson came indoors and sat half-on, half-against a table, as still as if he watched and listened to the movement of birds or animals. I saw and spoke with F. E. Smith (afterwards Lord Birkenhead) and H. G. Wells, with bishops, deans, the artist brothers Robinson (my friends thence-forward), Granville Fell, Herbert Railton, Arthur Symons, Ernest Rhys, later the editor of Everyman's Library, and many more. I read all the books I could lay my hands on, and there was no limit but that of time and strength and eyesight to this occupation. I heard Shaw, Belloc, and Chesterton speak and debate. I went to the galleries of many theatres, and saw everything, from *Othello* and *Rosmersholm* to *Old Heidelburg* and *The Light that Failed*. You will not wonder, there-fore, that in retrospect, when terrors and humiliations have been obliterated by time, this period seems to have been brimming with incalculable magic.

It was later, when I began to read manuscripts and advise for and against their publication, and when I began, also, to write books of my own, that I came into closer contact with authors, and learned their ways, their haunts, and their professional—sometimes their personal—secrets. I shall speak presently of authors. Here, I remark only that the publisher's undeclared view of authors, which I accepted from the first, long before I had published a book, is that they are unavoidable evils. It is not the view, held in rarefied circles, that quality is best proved by small sales. It is not the view, sometimes noticed in countries other than England, that the author is a person of importance. On the contrary, what publishers believe is that on the whole books would be better if they had no human appendages at all, especially female appendages, who are more tiresome than the other sort. Moreover, publishers do not like small sales, although one publisher did once say to another publisher, when asked if a book was doing well, that it was "having the best sort of success." The publisher to whom this was said, I remember, was considerably amused.

My own view of authors is not quite that of the publisher. Nor is it that of the authors. I have seen these unfortunate creatures from, as it were, both sides of the counter. I have laboured at the composition of books which were afterwards praised, disparaged, or ignored, which were unsuccessful, moderately successful, and, astonishingly, very successful indeed. I have handled thousands of such books when they were written by other men, sometimes with high hopes, sometimes with scepticism. And, like Dr Johnson, "my judgement I have found is no certain rule as to the sale of a book." A few good books do not sell; many bad books do sell; but since the majority of the books published are neither very good nor very bad, in spite of the desperate dreams of authors and the vagaries of reviewers, I think there is a kind of rough justice in the fates of most of them. They sell if people like them and recommend them to others; otherwise they are like men, of whom it has been said that "one may steal a horse, while another may not look over the hedge."

I did not know this when I moved from Dents, in Bedford Street, to Chatto and Windus, publishers of Swinburne, Stevenson, Walter Besant, James Payn, Ouida, and the early Arnold Bennett, in St Martin's Lane. I was astonished, then, to find that authors whom I supposed to sell in tens of thousands were lucky if they did in fact sell

Holywell Street

A Stall in St Anne Street, Soho
Victorian Haunts

A Victorian Newsboy

in tens of hundreds. I discovered that the so-called popular author, about whom lofty minds make lofty and inaccurate generalisations, was both less successful and more agreeable than I had expected. I found that my idols were first of all human beings, with the faults of ordinary men and a few extra faults which might be thought to compensate for their superior talents. I was forced to make various adjustments in my attitude towards books, writers, publishers, booksellers, and the reading public. I became more sophisticated, less of an amateur, and more and more detached from enthusiasm. It is unfortunate, but I fear inevitable, that experience should have these effects.

Nevertheless, as I survey the journey I have described in the foregoing pages, the journey from Farringdon Road to Paternoster Row and Holywell Street (Holywell Street, very narrow and, as I recall it, full of unwashed windows, was parallel with the Strand, in the vanished network of streets now replaced by Aldwych and the island between Aldwych and the Strand), and from Holywell Street to Covent Garden, and from Covent Garden to St Martin's Lane, Soho, and beyond, I find myself back in old states of mind. I venerate as I always did my seniors, Shaw, Belloc, Chesterton, Bennett, and Wells, and think they had a greatness in their approach to life, as well as greatness of talent, which is no longer possible in this era of dogmas, bigotries, and scheming self-advertisement. I live again the delights of seeing plays, by Ibsen, Chekhov, Shaw, Granville Barker, St John Hankin, and Barrie, which were modern at the beginning of the century. I recover a modest rivalry with my literary friends and contemporaries, such as Compton Mackenzie and Hugh Walpole. And I wish I could re-create for you the scene amid which books have been written and published during the last fifty years.

I cannot do this. It would lead me into writing the social and political history of half a century, which would enlarge the present book beyond measure. But I will tell you what I can, within limits; and shall borrow the words of other men to grace, diversify, and authenticate what might otherwise be what Pooh Bah called "a bald and unconvincing narrative." If I still fail, please to blame the instrument. The story itself is a rich one; and for me, as a memory, superlatively entertaining.

II

Some London Authors

1 *Authors who were not Londoners*

It is a mistake, cherished by those who can see no farther than their own doings, to suppose that English critical opinion is dictated from London. One has only to travel beyond sophistication to find that the Provinces have their own standards. Whether these standards are what the elegant would call provincial (that word is used in a very damning sense), or whether they are merely less fashionable (using that word, also, in a damning sense, as the equivalent of snobbish)*, I shall not try to determine. But I am sure that fashion does count for comparatively little in the Provinces, where men are less impressed by smartness; and I am sure that there are more things in heaven and earth than are dreamed of in London drawing-rooms. All the same, authors come to London.

They come to London because if most of the books are sold outside the town most of them are published within its limits. So young authors must travel here in order to see publishers. They then see other authors, their seniors or their rivals; and fall into cliques or solitudes; and a few of them make those social reputations which are very helpful—in London—to literary fame. Not all of them learn anything about London, because the literary world is a small one and many members of it know only their own small streets and limited horizons. But they help to make London history, and have their place in this book. In Chelsea, in St. John's Wood, in Bloomsbury and Soho; in fact everywhere within a two-mile radius of Broadcasting House, their words are golden. They come from Ireland, from Scotland, and from Wales; they come from Yorkshire and Cornwall and the Midlands. They adopt, and sometimes sweep, the town.

Shakespeare himself was no Londoner. Samuel Pepys was from Brampton in Huntingdonshire. Ned Ward, the *London Spy*, came from Oxfordshire, and John Gay, whose *Trivia* gave the picture of London as seen by an eighteenth-century pedestrian, belonged to Barnstaple. Dr Johnson travelled up from Lichfield, in Staffordshire, with,

* "Fashion is gentility running away from vulgarity, and afraid of being overtaken by it. It is a sign the two things are not very far asunder".—Hazlitt, *Conversations of James Northcote*.

12

according to his own teasing pleasantry at Garrick's expense, a penny more than Garrick's three-halfpence in his pocket. Charles Dickens was born at Landport in Portsea, Hampshire, and spent his earliest boyhood in Chatham. George Gissing came from Wakefield, in Yorkshire, by way of Manchester. Pett Ridge, whose cockney novels delighted a former generation, was from Canterbury; and Neil Lyons, that master of London speech, from as far away as South Africa. One and all settled here, for the profit of mankind; but they were not natives.

This may surprise you, because (so powerfully have they, by their writings, illuminated the scenes and manners of our city, and so much are they identified with particular ages in its history) most people assume them, with the exception of Shakespeare, to have been London born and bred. We gain our strongest impressions of Whitehall and Cheapside, the Great Plague and the Great Fire, from Pepys' daily records (I shall speak later of Defoe); the whole range of London life in the eighteenth century is spread before us in Boswell's *Johnson* and his more recently published *London Journal*; Dickens is the novelist *par excellence* of mid-nineteenth century London, as Gissing is the novelist of London in the eighteen-eighties; and I do not know of any better pictures of cockney manners in the twentieth century than one may find in the stories of Neil Lyons, with their original and delightful exactitudes and euphemisms for common oaths.

Has London any veritable sons to set against these as portrait painters of the city? Not, I think, more than half-a-dozen; and half-a-dozen only if one follows Hazlitt's example and describes Hogarth as a comic writer. The first of them is Ben Jonson, who is said to have been born in Westminster. The second is Thomas Dekker, whose play, *The Shoe-maker's Holiday*, is of as true London fashion as Jonson's *Bartholomew Fair*, and whose descriptions of Elizabethan London in *The Gul's Horn-booke* and *The Bel-man of London* are equal to anything we have ever had in that distinctive kind of writing. The third is Daniel Defoe, whose birth-place and home were close by Moorgate, and whose travels, real and imaginary, carried him all over England, all over Europe, and at last as he grew old and reached the zenith of his genius, all over the world. The fourth, who came long after these others, was W. W. Jacobs.

2 *A Dip into the Past*

Before I say another word on this theme I should like, for the sake of historical perspective, to take you back for a few minutes into the past, when London was a city within walls and gates, beyond which, to John Stow's indignation (Stow himself was a Londoner), there already spread, "pestering both sides of the street," "cottages and alleys, even up to Whitechapel Church, and almost half a mile beyond it, into the common field; all of which ought to be open and free to all men."

This Elizabethan London, where Shakespeare walked, where strawberries grew in the gardens of the Bishops of Ely in Holborn, and where, in another garden at Old Ford, one of Dekker's heroines astonishingly made her lover a garland of pinks, roses, violets, marigolds, and blushing gilliflowers, was perhaps not the London known to Chaucer. But it was a London hardly changed since the days of the Reformation; and men were alive in Shakespeare's day who could tell stories, if only at second-hand, of the Wars of the Roses, Perkin Warbeck, Wolsey, Anne Boleyn, and Thomas Cromwell. They were no more remote than the Crimean War, Gladstone, Garibaldi, or the Third Napoleon are to ourselves; or than Hitler, Mussolini and Winston Churchill will be to our grandchildren. Oral tradition, also, was stronger than it is today, when newspapers and the radio have riddled men's personal memories with uncertainty.

Furthermore, however much the thoroughfares of London may have changed in appearance, their lines and names were the same then as they are now. The Temple, Lincoln's Inn, and Gray's Inn stood as they stand today and have stood through the intervening centuries. A topographer-antiquary could conduct us about the town, reviving history as we went with snatches from not only the commentators Stow and Gerard, but such wits and playwrights as Jonson, Shakespeare, and Dekker. We, less learned, might hear only the noisy traffic of today; but if, afterwards, we turned to the authors he quoted, we too could travel back nearly four centuries in a few hours and see London as Elizabethan Londoners saw and loved it.

I do not want to sentimentalise the notion. I wish only to remind you that poets from Donne to Walter de la Mare have walked the same streets. The Mermaid Tavern was in Bread Street, Cheapside, and could be reached by passages from Cheapside and Friday Street. The Bear Garden, the Rose Theatre, the Swan, and the Globe were all directly across the river from Blackfriars or other points near and east of St Paul's. Although within the walls—which one can imagine by reference to the names of the various gates such as Ludgate, Newgate, Aldersgate, and the rest—older mansions had been discarded by rich men living safely in new great houses along the Strand, in the Savoy, and about Whitehall, the mansions had become tenements for those of lesser wealth, and continued as records of history. That is one reason why we read of Shakespeare residing in the parish of St Helen's, Bishopsgate, and why, to the Londoner of the twentieth century, the names of Cornhill, the Strand, Ludgate Hill, Lombard Street, and the Savoy are equally familiar as part of his heritage.

I imagine few theatregoers then ventured much with print; and yet, since it is of the bookman's London that I write, it seems only right that I should tell how printers and stationers, the latter being what we might call booksellers or publishers, or both, prospered in London streets. I am not very clear as to their practices in those days; but the Stationers' Company already existed, for it had applied for a royal charter of incorporation under King Henry VIII and received it from his daughter Mary. Also printers suffered lively prosecutions throughout the century for acts of independence or frivolity. And in accordance with universal practice books were printed and sold "at the sign of," which made the shops of booksellers as truly places of refreshment as taverns. What a pity that refreshment should now be pragmatically condemned as "escape"!

The sign habit was maintained in after centuries, and we see pleasant and otherwise meaningless vestiges of it in those windmills and sundials and watergates and borzois which amuse us on current title-pages. But in Elizabethan and Jacobean times the stationers, having no street-numbers, were more in earnest with their signs than modern publishers have time to be. To take a few simple instances, Thomas Thorpe, said by Sir Sidney Lee to be the "T.T." of the dedication to *Shakespeare's Sonnets*, published "at the Sign of the Tiger's Head in St Paul's Churchyard"; Blount, another of Shakespeare's publishers, "at the Sign of the Black Bear" in the same place; Hugh Singleton, "dwelling in Creede Lane, near unto Ludgate," used "the Sign of the Gylden Tunne"; William Ponsonby, again of St Paul's Churchyard, "the Sign of the Bishop's Head"; and Henry Herringman "the Sign of the Anchor, in the lower-walk of the New Exchange."

This last-named publisher has no place in the Elizabethan scene, because he lived under Charles I; but it was he who first printed John Donne's name in full upon the title-page of Donne's Poems. Previously the poems had been the work of J.D., and in Donne's lifetime hardly any of them had been published at all. Their circulation had been

15

in manuscript. Yet Ben Jonson told Drummond of Hawthornden in 1618–19 that Donne was, in some things, the first poet in the world. "His verses of the Lost Chain he hath by heart."

That is generous testimony from one who was not invariably generous, even about Donne, whom he would have hanged for "not keeping of accent." Does it perhaps emphasise the fact that in Queen Elizabeth's day men of letters lived very close to one another, observing rival genius (I say nothing about competitive dramatists) with little rancour? If you think time has softened the rancour, at least grant the inevitable nearness in a small city, before publicity was organised, and when literary murder was a matter for principals only.

3 *John Donne and Ben Jonson*

I should not like to say, and fortunately in this book am not called upon to discuss, whether Ben Jonson or John Donne was the greater writer. Obviously Jonson is the larger figure (not only physically); but Donne had a rarer refinement of genius. It was perceived by all who knew him, before a line of his poetry had been printed; and the intensity of his private reputation is so remarkable, both in itself and as the example of a phenomenon running all through the history of English literature, that I emphasise it. Donne, that is, was the aristocrat; Jonson the professional. Jonson was in the literary hurly-burly, big, rough-speaking, and prolific; Donne had no contact with that hurly-burly, but only with great men; and in his poems was concerned with himself, his passionate love for his wife, and, subsequently, his equally passionate austerity of faith. Little else; although the subtleties of his mind and heart were exquisite.

He was "moderately tall," "highly passionate," and capable of "winning behaviour,—which, when it would entice, had a strange kind of elegant irresistible art." He loved London. I do not know whereabouts in it he was born, because nobody knows; but Izaak Walton, his friend and biographer, says that the year of his birth was 1573, and that his father was a rich London merchant of good Welsh blood. His mother was of the family of Sir Thomas More. He was taught at home until he was ten, spent four years at the University of Oxford, and three at Cambridge; after which, being seventeen years of age, he inherited a fortune, studied law, was lured into theological speculation, and, travelling abroad with the frustrated intention of visiting Palestine, spent or lost all his money.

16

However, he was quickly made chief secretary to the Lord Chancellor of that day, and seemed destined to great employment for the State. Unluckily—at least, Walton says unluckily—he fell in love with the daughter of one who already held great employment, the Chancellor of the Garter and Lieutenant of the Tower. The lovers eloped. Thereupon Donne and his conspiring friends were thrown into prison, the lady was recovered by her father, and all hope of an important civil career was ended.

"I began early [the poet wrote], when I understood the study of our laws; but was diverted by leaving that, and embracing the worst voluptuousness, an hydroptic immoderate desire of human learning and language: beautiful ornaments indeed to men of great fortune, but mine was grown so low as to need an occupation; which I thought I entered well into, when I subjected myself to a service as I thought might exercise my poor abilities: and there I stumbled, and fell too."

He fell; but always among the great. He lived for years with a friend in Surrey; then, after lodging by himself near Whitehall while his family stayed at Mitcham, he was accommodated, with his family, in another friend's mansion in Drury Lane. And, since in those days all patronage radiated from the sovereign, James I came further to his rescue, persuading him with much difficulty to take orders, appointing him his own Chaplain in Ordinary, commanding Cambridge to make him an honorary Doctor of Divinity, appointing him Vicar of St Dunstan's in the West, and at last giving him the Deanery of St Paul's, a post which he held until his death in early middle age.

To the very end of his life Donne was treated as a superior being. He had no need, as lesser men had, to seek and flatter a patron. Since he was a commoner without estate he was not entirely independent; but as far as a commoner could be so he was free to follow the light of his own intellect and (always with due regard to the king's power) to act in accordance with his own paramount impulse. He withheld his early, passionate love poems from publication; he became a fervid preacher and an ascetic; but, as you have seen, Jonson and of course others considered him the first poet of the age. This is the earliest instance known to me in English literature—though Philip Sidney may provide another—of private, social literary reputation. It can be paralleled, in the case of lesser men, today.

Ben Jonson was born in the same year as Donne; but he had no Walton to record, with piety, the story of his life. Nor, in his youth, had he great associates. Nor, as one sees him, did he place any hope in noble patrons, although James I let him have a small pension and Charles I gave or promised him some help. What we know is a patch-work of legend, brag, and inference; and only John Aubrey, who claimed to have had the facts from an uncle, can tell you of two parts of London where Jonson is known to have lived in manhood. Aubrey's uncle said vaguely that "it was without Temple Bar, at a comb-maker's shop, about the Elephant and Castle," and that "in his later time" Jonson lived in Westminster, "in the house under which you pass as you go out of the churchyard into the old palace; where he died."

I can add to this only that, as is clear from Jonson's plays, the town, in one sense, belonged to him; that the dedication of *Volpone* is dated "from my house in the Black-friars"; and that his fortunes were always uncertain and his end harassed as much by poverty as a ruined carcase. A Scotsman by descent, and of an unruly tongue and temper, he was too strongly gifted not to arouse rivalry and dislike among others following the uncertain trade of letters.

"He was (it is again Aubrey who speaks) of a clear and fair skin; his habit was very plain. I have heard Mr Lacy, the player, say that he was wont to wear a coat like a coachman's coat with slits under the armpits. He would many times exceed in drink (Canary was his beloved liquor), then he would tumble home to bed, and, when he had thoroughly perspired, then to study. I have seen his study-ing chair, which was of straw, such as old women used, and as Aulus Gellius is drawn in . . . . He had one eye lower than the other, and bigger, like Clun, the Player."

Jonson's birthplace was Westminster. He was the son of one who, having offended against the laws of Queen Mary, lost whatever estate he had and died before the birth of his son. The widow then married a builder, living in Hartshorn Lane, near Charing Cross (according to Fuller), which was afterwards Northumberland Street. It is said that Ben was apprenticed to the trade of bricklaying. Perhaps in building walls he drew a lesson in form for another craft, regarding which he pointedly said that it is "the disease of the unskilful to think rude things greater than polished."

His own plays were certainly planned with care and polished with something more than their wit; a scrupulous craftsmanship so famous among other dramatists, and those attending the theatres, that it was made a ground of public mockery.

Ben Jonson

John Donne

Daniel Defoe in the Pillory : a Victorian reconstruction after E. Crowe

James Boswell

Joseph Addison

Leigh Hunt

Horace Walpole

But before coming to the theatre, first as player and then as inexhaustible dramatist, Jonson went to the Low Countries as a soldier,
returning ripe, stout, penniless, and boastful. He collaborated as playwright with other playwrights, quarrelled with his collaborators,
killed a man in a scuffle and was imprisoned and branded for the act,
and had *Every Man in His Humour* accepted and performed in 1598
by Shakespeare's company, the Lord Chamberlain's players.

In its first production *Every Man in His Humour*, according to a
convention of the period, was about Italians in an Italian city. But in
fact Jonson's comedies were always London comedies:

> Our scene is London, 'cause we would make known
> No country's mirth is better than our own.

They were packed with local and topical references, to "the Dagger
in Holborn," "the musters of Mile End," "Drake's old ship at Dept-
ford," "Pan of Belsize, and Clench the leech of Hampstead," and to
streets and taverns recognisable by any audience—Finsbury, Totten
Court, Old Jewry, Coleman Street, or, in *Bartholomew Fair*, to

> "these pretenders to wit! your Three Cranes, Mitre, and Mermaid
> men! not a corn of true salt, not a grain of right mustard amongst
> them all. They may stand for places, or so, against the next wit-
> fall, and pay two pence in a quart more for their canary than other
> men. But give me the man can start up a justice of wit out of six
> shillings beer, and give the law to all the poets and poet-suckers
> in town:—because they are the players' gossips!"

They were London comedies, for London audiences, filled with quips
as verbally adroit, and as immediately understood, as anything in a
modern revue. But they were also, the author claimed, realistic:

> He rather prays you will be pleas'd to see
> One such today, as other plays should be;
> Where neither chorus wafts you o'er the seas,
> Nor creaking throne comes down the boys to please;
>
> .   .   .   .
>
> But deeds, and language, such as men do use,
> And persons, such as comedy would choose.

There spoke the Londoner! Form, realism, wit, tremendous verve
and skill, and a deliberate exposure of boisterous London life in all its
coarse chicane were combined with insistence on the vanities, vagaries,

"humours," and fixed ideas of men in general. Few writers have had a greater impact on the literature current in their times. Jonson resembled a robust consolidation of Dickens and Bernard Shaw; and, as if to show prophetically that he would be beyond those men, he proved himself a classical scholar and a poet as well. He was moralist and extrovert, as Donne was casuist, sensualist, and metaphysician. The year which gave birth to both of them was a year of miracle.

4 *Dekker; the decline of the Patron*

Middleton, Marston, Massinger, Webster, Munday, Daniel, and Drayton; these and others played their parts in creating the drama which is one of the glories of Elizabethan—of London—literature.

Thomas Dekker

But of the whole assembly I propose to discuss only one, less because of his work for the theatre than because of several unique prose narratives or satires.

Thomas Dekker, wild, careless, and improvident, of whom Lamb said that he "had poetry enough for any thing," wrote *The Gul's Horn-Booke* and *Lanthorne and Candle-light*. He may have been the son of a Dutchman, and apprenticed to the trades of shoemaking or tailoring. It is certain that he was London-born. "O thou beautifullest daughter of two united Monarchies!" said he in *The Seven Deadly Sins of London*: "From thy womb received I my being, from thy breasts my nourishment!" He could have added, but did not do so: "From thy prisons, theatres, and taverns I learned all that I know of Life!" Yet the speeches of Jane, in *The Shoemaker's Holiday*, are among the really beautiful simplicities in dramatic literature; and I need not remind you, I am sure, that Dekker wrote a poem extolling contentment.

"The theatre," he says, instructing his Gul or Gallant in true London behaviour, "is your Poets' Royal Exchange. . . .

"Sithence then the place is so free in entertainment, allowing a stool as well to the Farmer's son as to your Templar, . . . let our Gallant presently advance himself up to the throne of the Stage. I mean not into the Lords' room (which is now but the Stage's Suburbs): No, those boxes, by the iniquity of custom, conspiracy of waiting-women and Gentlemen-Ushers, that there sweat together, and the covetousness of Sharers, are contemptibly thrust into the rear, and much new satin is there damned, by being smothered to death in darkness. But on the very Rushes where the Comedy is to dance, yea, and under the state of *Cambises* himself, must our feathered Ostrich, like a piece of Ordnance, be planted valiantly (because impudently) beating down the mews and hisses of the opposed rascality . . . .

"By sitting on the stage, you may (without travelling for it) at the very next door ask whose play it is; and, if you know not the author, you may rail against him: and peradventure so behave yourself, that you may enforce the Author to know you. . . .

"Now, sir, if he be a fellow that hath either epigrammed you, or hath had a flirt at your mistress, or hath brought either your feather, or your red beard, or your little legs &c. on the stage, you shall disgrace him worse than by tossing him in a blanket, or giving him the bastinado in a Tavern, if, in the middle of his play, (be it Pastoral or Comedy, Moral or Tragedy) you rise with a screwed and discontented face from your stool to be gone."

The gallant's instruction is not yet complete, however:

"I could now fetch you about noon . . . out of your chamber, and carry you with me into *Paul's Churchyard*; where, planting yourself in a Stationer's shop, many instructions are to be given you, what books to call for, how to censure of new books, how to mew at the old, how to look in your tables and inquire for such and such *Greek, French, Italian,* or *Spanish* Authors, whose names you have there, but whom your mother for pity would not give you so much wit as to understand."

Have we met the Gallant recently? I think we have. He goes no longer to St Paul's Churchyard; but his censure, his mewing, and his pretentiousness are modernity itself!

St Paul's Churchyard, I must explain, was the haunt of all Londoners in Elizabethan days, as it was, at lunchtime, in my boyhood, when it was the strolling-resting-ground of all who made their midday meal of sandwiches or bread-and-butter, or even peardrops and a cup of water from a fountain. In Dekker's day lunches were also eaten there; and if one had no lunch one was said to dine with Duke Humphrey, the celebrated patron of starvelings. The St Paul's of Queen Elizabeth was not our Wren church, but an older erection, and its aisles were sanctuary for debtors, swaggerers, and the pretentious riff-raff. "There," said Dekker, "you may spend your legs in winter a whole afternoon; converse, plot, laugh, and talk any thing, jest at your Creditor, even to his face, and in the evening, even by lamplight, steal out, and so cozen a whole covy of abominable catch-polls."

There were questionable bookmen in those days. Dekker, knowing all about them, in one chapter of *Lanthorne and Candle-light* described "a new kind of hawking." Two men, he said, would call upon some gentleman and insist on seeing him about important business. Then the first would say:

"Sir I am a poor Scholar, and the report of your virtues hath drawn me hither, venturously bold to fix your worthy name as a patronage to a poor short discourse which here I dedicate (out of my love) to your noble and eternal *Memory*. . . ."

"The *Hawking pamphleteer* is then bid to put on, whilst his *Miscellane Maecenas* opens a book fairly apparelled in vellum with gilt fillets and four penny silk ribbon at least, like little streamers on the top of a Marchpane Castle, hanging dandling by at the four corners. The title being superficially surveyed in the next leaf he sees that the *Author* hath made him one of his Gossips: for the book carries his worship's name, and under it stands an Epistle just the length of a Henchman's grace before dinner."

In consequence of this affecting sight, the flattered dedicatee would give money, and perhaps a meal to the author; who proceeded to another gull with another appropriately dedicated copy of the book.

You see what has happened. The great patron, who pressed purses into the hands of genius and gave that genius friendship and countenance, is yielding to the inferior patron, a minor Maecenas coveting

22

humbler flatteries and granting smaller doles. Dedications are to be catchpenny.

"This new kind of Hawking can afford no name unless 5 be at it, viz.
1. He that casts up the *Lure* is called the *Falconer*.
2. The Lure that is cast up is an idle *Pamphlet*.
3. The *Tercel Gentle* that comes to the Lure is some knight or some gentleman of like quality.
4. The *Bird* that is preyed upon, is Money.
5. He that walks the horses, and hunts dry foot, is called a *Mongrel*.

The Falconer having scraped together certain small parings of wit, he first cuts them handsomely in pretty pieces, and of those pieces does he patch up a book. This book he prints at his own charge, the *Mongrel* running up and down to look to the workmen, and bearing likewise some part of the cost (for which he enters upon his half-share). When it is fully finished, the *Falconer* and his *Mongrel* (or it may be two *Falconers* join in one) . . . devise what Shire in *England* it is best to forage next . . . printing of so many epistles as they have names; the epistles Dedicatory being all one, and vary in nothing but the titles of their patrons."

So vanity was exploited. The Elizabethan sharp was blood brother to the publishing sharp of yesterday, who told authors their work was excellent, and demanded forty or fifty pounds towards the cost of printing it. Dekker has exposed for us all, with cockney good humour, what would now be called a ramp. Observe that he does it with relish, as Jonson exposes his rogues, fools, and humbugs; and with no rancour whatever. One sees him smiling. Does this fact link him in your eyes with W. W. Jacobs?

5 *Defoe; London a city of merchants; the Plague*

I do not know whether Defoe ever laughed. I know he was an extraordinary man, a man of genius. I know that when he wrote *The Shortest Way with Dissenters* he is said (though George Saintsbury would have none of this) to have been mocking his opponents with a gravity equal to Swift's gravity when he wrote *A Modest Proposal for Preventing the Children of Poor People from being a Burthen to Their Parents or the Country* (which was that they should, in Ireland, be used for food). But, with all admiration, I cannot recognise in Defoe's writings anything but dry gravity.

He had an immense interest in material things. He travelled all over England and Scotland as a secret agent for Robert Harley, Earl of Oxford, when that ambiguous statesman was bent on discovering the mind of the nation; and his famous *Tour* is an incomparable source-book for students of the eighteenth century. He gave the lead to Steele and Addison by establishing *The Review*; and he was father of the realistic novel, that sober lying in which one cannot distinguish between fact and fiction. Yet in all this, apart from intrepidity and freedom from illusions, the only specifically cockney characteristic is

Defoe's House at Tooting

irony. I do not claim Defoe, therefore, as a typical Londoner; much as I should like to do so.

He is one of the literary glories of London. He is one of the most serious critics of Londoners, too. In his *Tour* he remarks disapprovingly the effect upon the lives of surrounding countrymen of the giant greed of London for their produce. His picture of Londoners in face of the horrors of the Plague is ungenial. His most famous heroine, who declares that she is well known at Newgate and the Old Bailey, has no morals whatever and finds that the men she meets in town are equally unprincipled. Only in his steadfast nonconformity and refusal to lie down under imprisonment, the pillory, bankruptcy, or the legends of liars and romantic historians, does he show decided character. Otherwise he was an opportunist, a hack writer, a spy, a not always honourable investor and merchant, and a genius. Some clue to such contradictions is missing.

He was born in or about 1660, and may just have been old enough at the time of the Plague and Fire of London to gather childish but terrible impressions of both these calamities. His father was a tallow-chandler who lived in Fore Street, by Moorgate, one of the parts of London devastated by German fire-bombs in the late war; and Defoe was brought up a Presbyterian. Those were days when the accumulation of wealth in trade was an English preoccupation; and Defoe, who as a young man wanted to make his fortune quickly, became a merchant. He dealt in haberdashery, tobacco, ships, bricks and tiles, and civet cats. But circumstances were against him; by the time he was thirty-three he owed seventeen thousand pounds and could not pay them.

He therefore had to find other means of growing rich. Some of these were political; they took him into journalism and pamphleteering, trouble and prosecution and punishment: "Earless on high," wrote Pope, "stands unabash'd Defoe."

At last he entered the true field for his genius, by which he has ever since been known to the world. But he did not write *Robinson Crusoe* until he was nearly sixty. Otherwise his approach in everything he did was commercial. "The main affair of life," he said, speaking for his mercantile age, "is getting money."

When we read the *Tour* or the *Essay on Projects*, we understand how much consideration he had given to this main affair; but when we read his extraordinary *Journal of the Plague Year* it is to discover a different concern. He was devoted to facts..If he could not acquire them, he invented them; but I think it certain that in his picture of London he used material made available by the records of an uncle. How otherwise could he have ventured so many verifiable details? He tells how, in September 1664, rumours reached England that the Plague was returned to Holland; and adds:

> "we hoped it was not true; till the latter End of November, or the beginning of December 1664, when two men, said to be French men, died of the Plague in Long Acre, or rather at the upper End of Drury Lane."

He then prints official figures of burials in the local parishes of St

Giles's in the Fields and St Andrew's, Holborn, to show how deaths rose, slackened, and rose alarmingly.

"The Distemper was spread into two or three other Parishes (viz) St Andrew's, Holborn, St Clement's Danes, and to the great Affliction of the City, one died within the Walls, in the Parish of St Mary-Wool-Church, that is to say, in Bearbinder-lane near the Stocks-market."

"I lived without Aldgate about mid-way between Aldgate Church and White-Chappel-Bars, on the left Hand or North-side of the Street; and as the Distemper had not reach'd to that Side of the City, our Neighbourhood continued very easy. But at the other End of the Town, their consternation was very great; and the richer sort of People, especially the Nobility and Gentry, from the West-part of the City throng'd out of Town, with their Families and Servants. . . . Indeed nothing was to be seen but Waggons and Carts, with Goods, Women, Servants, Children, &c., Coaches fill'd with People of the better Sort, and Horsemen attending them, and all hurrying away."

I expect you noticed the cunning hesitation of "the latter End of November, or the beginning of December," and the precision of Bearbinder Lane and "the left Hand or North-side of the street." Such precision is not what used to be called "meticulous," but arises from a richness or plenitude of enthusiasm for fact. Ask a cockney when anything happened to him; he will stir his memories, will venture a day, will correct himself: "Wensday. No, I'm a liar; it was Thursday. Yes, Thursday. Sem o'clock. No. fi'parce. Fi'parce sem, Thursday." Thereafter there is no shaking him.

At the time of the Plague, says Defoe, "we had not such things as printed newspapers, to spread rumours and reports of things; and to improve them by the invention of men, as I have lived to see practised since." But there had been an increase in popular reading.

"The people were more addicted to Prophecies, and Astrological Conjurations, Dreams, and old Wives' Tales, than ever they were before or since. . . . Books frightened them terribly; such as Lilly's Almanack, Gadbury's Alogical Predictions; Poor Robbin's Almanack and the like; also several pretended religious Books, one entituled, 'Come out of her My People, least you be partaker of her Plagues;' another call'd Fair Warning; another Britains Remembrancer, and many such."

Here, too, are words to startle all among us who, during the Second World War, spent days or nights in London:

"It is true, a vast many People fled, as I have observ'd; . . . such People as were unincumbred with Trades and Business: But of the rest, the Generality stay'd, and seem'd to abide the worst. . . . It is indeed to be observ'd, that the Women were in all this Calamity, the most rash, fearless, and desperate Creatures."

So much for Defoe.

6 *W. W. Jacobs; H. G. Wells; G. K. Chesterton; the London poets; Disraeli*

I always intended to return to W. W. Jacobs, the fourth of my London authors. You remember Jacobs? He has discovered a new vitality on the radio, where his longer stories are read to us as "serials"; and his books are reprinted as they will continue to be reprinted until London is no more. He astonished natives of the town, and strangers also, in the eighteen-nineties, by way of several popular magazines, and was in time retained for the exclusive pleasure of readers of *The Strand*, already famous as the centre from which Sherlock Holmes spread to the wide world. He was in manner shy, retiring, and melancholy; but he knew the London he was born in, and although, at first, an unremarked clerk in the Post Office Savings Bank he told stories about London's bargees, longshoremen, and retired captains which will be immortal.

Londoners had just then been re-discovered as a theme by men engrafting upon *Oliver Twistian* narratives the strictness of French realism. The books of these men, written later than Gissing's *The Unclassed*, *Thyrza*, *A Life's Morning*, and *The Nether World*, specialised in mean streets, primitive passions, tragedies by gaslight, and social contrasts. Jacobs did not so specialise. Though he wrote at first for the same periodicals as his contemporaries, he showed the true Londoner's unillusioned tolerance of sin, his dry amusement with small contretemps, his irony, and his preference for the implicit; and, if his field was small, he gave it universality. More, he converted it into fairyland.

He did this deliberately. Knowing every evil that the realists expounded, he toyed coolly, demurely, triflingly with naughty sailors as if their comedy were all he understood. He did this to such perfection that some saw him as no more than amiable. Yet none of the serious, the sociological, writers ever, when picturing London, surpassed him. I will not say that he was the greatest of London authors; I say that for all his fun he communicated, as the others could not do, the irrepressible spirit of silent mockery characterising those who are incapable of thinking of themselves as provincial.

Captain Bowers, in *Dialstone Lane*, observes, not for the first time, that a young woman has appeared within his bachelor home, in spite of the fact that his manservant, Tasker, has signed articles forswearing the company of females. He rings the bell.

"Has that young woman gone?" he inquired, cautiously, as Mr Tasker appeared.

"Yessir," was the reply.

"What about your articles?" demanded the Captain, with sudden loudness. "What do you mean by it?"

Mr Tasker eyed him forlornly. "It ain't my fault," he said, at last. "I don't want her."

"Eh?" said the other, sternly, "Don't talk nonsense. What do you have her here for, then?"

"Because I can't help myself," said Mr Tasker, desperately; "that's why. She's took a fancy to me, and, that being so, it would take more than you and me to keep 'er away."

"Rubbish," said his master.

Mr Tasker smiled wanly. "That's my reward for being steady," he said, with some bitterness: "that's what comes of having a good name in the place. I get Selina Vickers after me."

"You—you must have asked her to come here in the first place," said the astonished captain.

"*Ask* her?" repeated Mr Tasker, with respectful scorn. "*Ask* her? She don't want no asking."

"What does she come for, then?" inquired the other.

"Me," said Mr Tasker, brokenly. "I never dreamt o' such a thing. I was going 'er way one night—about three weeks ago, it was—and I walked with her as far as her road—Mint Street. Somehow it got put about that we were walking out. A week afterwards she saw me in Harris's, the grocer's, and waited outside for me till I come out and walked 'ome with me. After she came in the other night I found we was keeping company."

. . . . .

"Well, tell her I won't have her here," said the captain, rising. "Good night."

BLEAK HOUSE

BY

CHARLES DICKENS.

LONDON:

BRADBURY & EVANS BOUVERIE STREET

1853

A First Edition of 1853

"I've told her over and over again, sir," was the reply, "and all she says is she's not afraid of you, nor six like you."

The captain fell back silent, and Mr Tasker, pausing in a respectful attitude, watched him wistfully.

As you have seen, the captain is as much afraid of the lady as Tasker is, and with good reason; for Selina has character. Jacobs had seen many such girls in the course of his life; and by the grace of genius he was able to do them justice.

H. G. Wells, less consummately, in his lighter work did something similar. Wells was from a part of outer London. In boyhood he went farther from the centre; and as a young man he came back to Kensington, Camden Town, Dickens (a worn set of whose works, in the fine red square "Charles Dickens Edition," filled always a handy place on his bookshelves, with *Bleak House* the best-worn of them all), and, a little later, Hampstead. Wells was no typical Londoner; he was impatient, and he was troubled by memory of social inferiority in boyhood. These things are impossible to a cockney, who has no inferiorities. Wells may have tried to be a philosopher, as Doctor Johnson's friend did, and as the Londoner is by birthright; but something other than cheerfulness kept breaking in, and he went rampaging with an uneasy spirit in pursuit of change. Nevertheless he had the proper relish of impudent humour. When it was not overlaid by reforming zeal, this relish made him laugh as he wrote. Gilbert Chesterton, a Kensington product, also laughed as he wrote. Since authorship is a gloomy pastime, this is an uncommon characteristic.

Gilbert Chesterton is one of the London-born authors who made no pretence of portraying his native town. He came from what Leigh Hunt called "the Old Court Suburb," and he was as far as possible from being a cockney in spirit. His interest could not be in the living town, because it was in a magic Never-never Land of the Past, when England was young, and heaven was all about its simple-minded people. I will not say that William Morris, the Walthamstow-born Merrie Englander, was his inspiration; but the thought is less far-fetched than you may at first suppose. The maypole and the dancing bear were never far from Chesterton's thoughts; and the invisible postman in the Father Brown story was as near as he came to the anonymities of the city population. But his poetic fancy followed one of the great traditions of London, which has ever been a breeding-ground for poets.

It was so in the warrantable past. Langland was not a cockney;

Ouida (on a Cigarette Card)

Marie Corelli

George Eliot

Christina Rossetti

Victorian Women of Letters

Ambrose Bierce

Robert Hichens

Sir Edmund Gosse

George Augustus Sala

The Moustache in Literature

Hall Caine

Sir John Robinson

William Morris

Sir Walter Besant

The Beard in Literature

Clement Shorter and
Max Pemberton

Thomas Hardy

G. K. Chesterton

but some of his best scenes are laid in London. Chaucer was born here. So was Edmund Spenser. So were Herrick, Cowley, Milton, Pope, Gray, and William Blake. If Shakespeare's plays were written by Bacon, London would almost sweep the poetic board. Its fecundity is at least an added strength to the Baconian case. The Rossettis, both Christina and Dante Gabriel, were born in Charlotte Street, Portland Place; Robert Browning in Camberwell; Swinburne in Chester Street, Grosvenor Place. That small galaxy of great talents, only some of whom fell under Scots disapproval more than a hundred years ago as The Cockney School, but which included Charles Lamb, Byron, Keats, and Leigh Hunt, were Londoners to a man. What celestial cockneys! In themselves alone they would establish a claim that England has led the world in poetry for five and a half centuries!

Dare I mention, in such company, with only side glances at John Wilkes and John Ruskin, another genius who began to write rodomontade in the age of Lamb and Hazlitt, and who lived to be Prime Minister of Great Britain? Benjamin Disraeli, son of an ardent bookman, could never remember where he was born (he pretended to think it was in a library in the Adelphi), nor when his birthday was. Others knew, however, and unusually exact records had been kept of the event. The time was half-past five in the morning of Friday, December 21st, 1804; the place was a house now known as 22 Theobalds Road, Bloomsbury. You may see it marked with a plaque.

7 H. M. Tomlinson; the presentation of London; "a city of living men and women"

It is fitting that this chapter should end with some reference to a London-born writer who is still, at the moment of writing, actively engaged in portraying the spirit of the town in which he has spent more than seventy years of life. H. M. Tomlinson is not a Donne, nor a Jonson, nor a Dekker, nor a Defoe, nor a Jacobs. He is neither poet nor dramatist. He is not concerned, as Defoe was, with naked facts. He is less an annalist than an analyst. But he knows London, and he moves about her streets with the calm understanding of London life which a foreigner can never know.

Here, for instance, is a passage from his first novel, *Gallions Reach*, that tale of London and the world:

"There is a region of grey limestone and glass, horizontally stratified into floors, intersected by narrow ravines called avenues, and

honeycombed by shipping and commercial offices, which lies between Fenchurch and Leadenhall Streets. Billiter Avenue is one of its
intersecting clefts. This secluded corner of the city must be traversed
on foot, because its narrow paths were marked out only for its cliff
climbers; but nobody ever goes into it except they who are concerned with the secrets of its caves. The wealth of the cave of Sinbad,
compared with that of most of the offices in this canton of the city,
would have seemed but a careless disposal of the superfluous, yet
within the guarded recesses of the cliffs of Billiter Avenue no treasure
is ever visible. . . . Still, its virtue is there, powerful, though ab-
stract and incredible. The attraction of the hidden treasure of this
region, if as baffling to strangers as the beauty of the innumerable
brass name-plates at its doors, is dominant, nevertheless."

Something has happened, you see, to the portrayal of London by
its natives. To Ben Jonson and Dekker it was a beloved centre of riot,
chicane, humours, and mummery; still half-medieval. To Defoe it
was what it had become, a great mart where men found money-
getting the main affair of life, where poetry had had more than its ears
clipped, and where the generality of the population seemed stoically
to abide the worst. Ben Jonson had lampooned the puritans as humbugs; Dekker had laughed with that good-humour which today is
out of fashion at cheats, swaggerers, and users of taverns and ordinaries.
But between Jonson and Defoe the puritans had achieved power,
had been swept away by human longing for spice and colour, and had
lived, powerless but industrious, under the curse of innumerable
privations.

This series of events had left its consequences. The brilliant licence of
Congreve and Wycherley in the theatre had arisen and been driven
down again by moral pressure. A Protector and three kings had come
and gone. Defoe himself was of a puritan faith and had been partially
trained for the nonconformist ministry. His writing held no swagger,
and no colour, no fun, no brilliance; it was as plain as Roundhead
costume. Boisterous laughter, and what Taylor, the waterman-poet,
had called in Elizabethan days "this golden, stirring world," had given
place to merchanting and a love of facts. It was a sign that London itself
had changed.

Merriment was not long absent from the town; we had in Fielding
and Hogarth men who saw with the comic eye and ranged themselves
comfortably enough with Jonson and Dekker. They did, I think,

restore the true London spirit, although only Hogarth, who, appropriately, was born in Bartholomew Close, was a true cockney. Dickens followed, exaggerating, dramatising, but keeping ever before his readers' minds the dark corners and romantic alley-ways of the city. And as Victorian prosperity made Englishmen, and particularly Londoners, the mixture we know, it was left for strangers to describe the new ranks of society, the squalors of mean streets, the respectable humdrum of suburban millions, the profit-making manufacturers and traders, with the seriousness of students coming from good provincial homes and schools to survey the life of a great metropolis. Such writers were cultured, morally intent, foreign.

They generalised. It is not the cockney way. To Londoners all the qualities and defects of mankind are known—or are assumed. That is why, earlier, I said I thought W. W. Jacobs to be typical of the Londoner. I add now that H. M. Tomlinson is in his own way equally typical. He is shrewd, humorous, and incapable of the grandiose; but he has lived in and by the town, which is as familiar to him as his own hand, and he has also looked higher and farther than the town, as poets do, while yet walking its streets with a journalist's eye for their features.

He is more modern, less timeless, than Jacobs; and this means that he is more reflective. He has ever been more a man of thought than a man of action. This is why he takes the hero of *Gallions Reach* from that cave in Billiter Street out into Lime Street and past the offices of the Hudson's Bay Company, towards Leadenhall Street, where once Charles Lamb worked in the Offices of the East India Company, along Gracechurch Street (which was Grass Street in Stow's day), and on to London Bridge. There the young man pauses:

"He leaned on the parapet above British and Foreign Wharf and looked down to the plan of a steamer's deck. There was a smell of oranges. There was a ship. . . .

"London was too big to know itself. It was congested with anxious people and nervous engines, and at the same time a man might just as well be on Crusoe's island. The Angel Gabriel himself couldn't make a chart of London. . . . It was terrifying, if you thought about it. London was like the dream in which you stood by yourself at night and saw all the stars break loose and stream down the sky. . . . That dream, the stars out of law and falling down the sky, was like the spectacle of London on a Saturday afternoon."

The Londoner in such a mood no longer makes fun, nor observes trade; his mind has taken a cosmic journey. Tomlinson is a philosopher using London as a symbol of the universe.

"Londoners groping to their duties in a black-out, or working desperately by the glare of buildings alight, correcting tangles of tram cables, telephone wires and fire hose, patching the roof of a gasometer which has an unexploded bomb in its belly, stopping the floods of broken water-mains while the blasts continue, entering a furnace in the hope of saving people entrapped, and worse tasks, better not described, these men know there can be no recompense. No recompense at all. They are but salving the remains of a world which has passed; something with which to start another. . . . We are coming down to first things."

London has changed in three hundred and fifty years. It has been nearer total destruction than Ben Jonson and his contemporaries could ever have imagined. And Tomlinson wrote those words in the shadow of destruction. But you will have seen how simply he testifies in them to London pride and the spirit of her people. There is not much difference, really, between Dekker's cry of 1606, "O thou beautifullest daughter of two united Monarchies," and Tomlinson's quiet tribute to Londoners. In both is expressed the assurance that, as E. V. Lucas once observed, "London is before all things a city of living men and women."

III

Some London Publishers

1 *Parlous publishing; restraint in advertisement; publishers no scholars*

It is sometimes thought by authors that publishers hardly deserve the books they publish; but publishers think very differently. I once found a printed letter, copies of which had been sent to authors of rejected manuscripts in the eighteen-eighties. It gave, as an excuse for rejection, "the present parlous condition of the publishing trade." And however much the trade may seem to have changed in the last seventy years—and even in my time it has changed very markedly—in one respect it has remained just as it was. It is still "parlous." It has always been "parlous."

At its first beginning it was parlous because it was hampered by political and other restrictions. It is parlous today because the costs of production have risen so high that few books can be made to show a profit. Then and now, it has been and is parlous because no man can explain why one book sells and another fails to sell. Yet, as you can understand, it is upon the sales of the books he publishes that the publisher depends for a livelihood; and, more than this, it is on account of the profits he hopes to make from his larger-selling titles that the publisher takes the risk of publishing other works from which he expects to make no profit at all. The best-seller has critics; but in the past it has supported many a valuable worst-seller.

Back in Shakespeare's day, and again in the eighteenth century, publishers would band together to bear the costs of production. They did this with the First Folio of Shakespeare, when Jaggard, Smethwicke, Aspley, and Blount were joined. They did it even more imposingly with Johnson's *Lives of the Poets*, when no fewer than forty "of the most respectable booksellers of London" held a meeting and agreed to support an edition of the English Poets which Johnson should be asked to edit. But it has long been rare for two or more publishers to collaborate; and from the beginning of the nineteenth century until today much pride has been taken in the single imprints by which firms have established reputations for quality, responsibility, and success.

Whether members of the general public ever notice this imprint is questionable. Members of the general public often do not notice the names of the authors of their favourite books. But authors pay great heed to imprint; and a run of success in one publisher's list will often cause them to hasten to this publisher with their wares. They hope to prosper by infection.

Just what was the publishing world like when I first came into it? I have been looking at some of the old lists, and remarking how gently, how unobtrusively, books used then to slip into being; how Macmillan, Longmans, and John Murray would give, as it were, a hesitant cough, and observe with delicious laconism that on the following Thursday something would be published—something by "Mr Kipling," for example, "Mr Hardy," or "Mr Swinburne"—with no hint that the work was a masterpiece or that it was stupendous, magnificent, overwhelming, or even long-awaited. Such terms did not become the vogue until publishers grew desperate and began to raise their voices.

Indeed, in those days publishers waited for readers to buy their books. They actually waited for authors to bring them what we now know to have been magnificent or stupendous masterpieces. They sat in their offices; they wrote all their letters by hand, in copying ink which office-boys blurred by the use of wet linen sheets into ridiculous messes looking like the scamperings of a thousand sodden spiders; and they waited. Unsuccessful authors crept before them with manuscripts; successful authors were recognisable because they no longer crept; a beautiful quiet dignity pervaded the publishers. Many of them wore beards of silver.

You must not think of these older publishers as men of great wisdom or scholarship. The farther one goes back into the past to examine their doings the clearer it becomes that they were nothing of the sort. One of the famous Elizabethans, Andrew Maunsell, had been a draper. The first Dodsley was "raised from an obscure station in life," which means that before beginning to employ authors he had been a footman and a successful dramatist. Later in the eighteenth century Lackington, a journeyman shoemaker, deserted his last and originated the practice of buying "remainders," or those copies of a book which the original publishers altogether despaired of selling. He became a rich man.

Among more modern publishers, the Tinsleys, Edward and William, were the sons of a Hertfordshire gamekeeper; and Edward, when in drink, would confess to having come to London riding on top of a haycart. William, the younger, was said by George Moore to look like Thackeray's futile Mr Sedley and to be "quite witless and quite *h*-less." My own first book-publishing employer, J. M. Dent, who could not spell, had made his way into the trade from the binder's bench; my second, Andrew Chatto, though by no means illiterate, gave no sign of being a scholar, and indeed used to say enviously of any author who wrote grammatically that he "had the power of the pen." I do not suggest that any of these men was the worse publisher for his lack of formal education. I merely remark the fact, in order to draw a contrast between the old school and the new, which sometimes illustrates purposeful culture at its extreme.

This is one of the changes to occur in my time; it is a striking feature of this incalculable trade. The trade itself calls for a minimum of literacy. But it rightly attracts book-lovers, because with all its faults and follies it has a romantic interest denied to trades showing larger margins of profit. It may be true that publishers could not exist without authors, a fact which they sometimes forget; but I suspect that authors could not exist without publishers.

2 *Authors and Publishers: Vizetelly; the Tinsleys; early Hardy novels*

Authors do not like this state of affairs. Roger North, halfway through the eighteenth century, cried aloud that

"it is wretched to consider what pickpocket work, with the help of the press, these demi-booksellers make. They crack their brains to find out selling subjects, and keep hirelings in garrets, at hard meat, to write."

Worse still were Dryden's "upon trial I find all of your trade are sharpers," and a horrid description of the great Jacob Tonson:

> With leering look, bull-fac'd, and freckled fair,
> With two left legs, with Judas-coloured hair,
> And frowsy pores, that taint the ambient air.

Pope joined in the cry when he referred to "shameless Curll" and shameless Curll's mishaps, as the result of one of which

> Obscene with filth the miscreant lies bewray'd,
> Fallen in the plash his wickedness had laid.

But while few ever said a good word for Edmund Curll, who is universally known as "the unspeakable," and whom I shall not defend, it must be mentioned that Dryden's *jeu d'esprit* at Tonson's expense was the result of momentary friction over money, and that Pope's copied jest at Tonson's two left legs referred to the publisher of a translation of Homer which rivalled his own. Pope's abuse of Curll arises from a more intricate matter, in which actual piracy, and a plot between Pope and Curll to pretend a piracy, of Pope's letters had their share; it was, by anticipation, Pickwickian. So, probably, was the publisher's equally scurrilous retort.

Leaving Curll aside, however, as "unspeakable," there is no doubt that Tonson, Lintot, and Dodsley were the best as well as the most famous booksellers—*i.e.* publishers—of the eighteenth century. Their offices—Tonson was in the Strand, "at the Shakespeare's Head against Katherine Street"; Lintot (who published Pope's Homer) "at the Cross-Keys between the Temple Gates in Fleet Street"; and Dodsley "at Tully's Head in Pall Mall"—became noted meeting-places for authors. Tonson had a considerable hand in establishing the Kit-Kat Club, the members of which included, besides Steele, Congreve, and Addison, celebrated nobles of the day; and Dodsley's shop, standing where the Guaranty Trust now is, was a honey-pot. Until John Murray the Second entertained Byron, Tom Moore, Coleridge, and Walter Scott in his first premises in Fleet Street, and Taylor and Hessey, who published for Keats, Hazlitt, and De Quincey, gave famous parties in Waterloo Place, publishers—perhaps excepting only Davies, at whose home Boswell met Johnson— did not again assemble such literary galaxies. Nor, with the exception of George Doran, the American, have they done so since, apart from omnium gatherum cocktail parties.

You have seen these patrons of authorship called unspeakable, leering and frowsy. It is because authors were bound to have commercial dealings with them. John Wolcot, otherwise Peter Pindar, towards the end of his life sold his copyrights for an annuity; but he pretended that the purchasers made a practice of drinking from the skulls of authors. Charles Lamb, so often miscalled "gentle," complained of having been bilked by his publisher; and called the tribe "Turks and Tartars when they have poor authors at their beck." Byron had to be reminded by Murray that he was dealing with a gentleman. H. G. Wells once wrote across the top of a letter to an early publisher "Damned rascal you are!" And the story could be continued indefinitely. Only Johnson, who sold his Satires after Juvenal to a Dodsley for ten and fifteen guineas, and called him "Doddy," ever said a good word for the trade. He and Boswell while travelling together chatted of the difficulties of book-publishers; and honest Johnson remarked that he had found his own judgment no sure guide as to the success or otherwise of a book. He also said that a man who wrote for anything but money was a blockhead.

Alas, all authors, even those who turn up the whites of their eyes at the thought of commerce, secretly wish for fame and fortune. If they have fame, but no fortune, they scorn the fortunate; if they have fortune, but tarnished fame, they pine for rehabilitating failure. When, as is the case with most authors, they have neither fame nor fortune, they accuse their publishers of incompetence. Do not blame them overmuch for such folly.

Publishers have not always been as generous as they are today, when competition drives them almost crazy. Towards the end of the nineteenth century, owing to the small sales of books, shortage of capital, and a strong tendency towards over-trading, they grew—to authors—quite parsimonious. But then they were not noticeably competent; or they fell foul of the police by attempting to circulate realistic tales; or they were unlucky in missing the taste of the moment or in having quarrelsome authors who, at the slightest success, removed their books.

Vizetelly was one of the unlucky ones. His premises must have been near the site of Tonson's; for he was actually in Catherine Street, Strand. We owe him a great debt. He first, I think, introduced the chief Russian authors to the British public—before that public was ready for them;—and published translations of Tolstoy, Dostoevsky, and Lermontov. So far, so good! But I am sorry to say that he went too far. He tried to present, not only George Moore and Gautier, but unexpurgated Zola. It was this last act which was fatal to him.

The Tinsleys, whom I mentioned a page or two earlier, were also in Catherine Street. The elder of them was the better man; his junior was, I have heard, one of the rare Englishmen of those days unceremonious enough to work in his shirtsleeves. He was altogether unceremonious. Having to handle a business formed by his more gifted brother, he tried to overreach William Black, the novelist considered superior to Hardy by Justin McCarthy. Black, outwardly a mild man, said he would see Tinsley damned before he would accept the offer. "Very well," retorted Tinsley; "take your book to Hell with my compliments." As one would expect, Black's work at once triumphed in another publisher's list.

George Moore was very scathing about this younger Tinsley.

"There was a publisher in Catherine Street," said he, "who used to frequent a certain bar, and this worthy man conducted his business as he dressed himself, sloppily. . . . From long habit, he would make a feeble attempt to drive a bargain, but he was duped generally. If a fashionable author asked two hundred pounds for a book out of which he was certain to make three, it was ten to one that he would allow the chance to drift away from him; but after having refused a dozen times the work of a Strand loafer whom he was in the habit of 'treating,' he would say, 'Send it in, my boy, send it in, I'll see what can be done with it.' There was a long counter, and the way to be published by Mr Tinsley was to straddle on the counter and play with a black cat."

Moore himself straddled, and saw his brevities published in *Tinsley's Magazines*; but so did other men. One of these, Edmund Downey, who worked for Tinsley and became a publisher on his own account, wrote a book about literary life in the eighties which, being published in 1905, was called *Twenty Years Ago*. Here one may read a confession once made by Tinsley about Thomas Hardy:

"I remember Tom Hardy well when he first called on me. He told me he was an architect, but had given up the profession on account, I think, of some eye trouble. Anyhow, I tried his first novel, *Desperate Remedies*, in three volumes. It went very flat. The only decent review I can remember was in the *Saturday*. . . . I tried him again with a little book, *Under the Greenwood Tree*. I gave him five-and-twenty down* and got it into two volumes. He told me that he was a bit disappointed, but he meant to keep on—that he had always been studying the folk down in his country and had made notes enough about their queer sayings and doings to fill many volumes. . . . So his third book came along—*A Pair of Blue Eyes*. After running it in the magazine, I got it out in three volumes. There was no great money in it, but I could see that Hardy was going to get a grip some day. While *A Pair of Blue Eyes* was running through the magazine, Hardy called on me and said he wanted to be quite fair and candid with me. The editor of another magazine had written to him offering to take a novel from him, and this editor's firm was willing to give three hundred pounds for it. I

* A mistake. Tinsley bought the copyright for thirty pounds, and it was among the books bought from his list by Chatto & Windus, who in after years sold to Macmillans the right to include it in their uniform editions of Hardy.

William Tinsley, from a Caricature by F. Waddy

think it was three hundred—anyhow, it seemed too much money for me to give with my experience of him so far; so I thanked him very much and said, 'Take the offer, my boy. I couldn't spring so much.' I seem to be unlucky about fourth novels, for the one I declined was *Far from the Madding Crowd*!"

After this, you will not be surprised to learn that the last time George Moore saw Tinsley's chair "it was standing in the street in the hands of the brokers." Moore did not express regret at the sight; he must have felt as Lamb did when he wrote:

> What should we do when Booksellers break?
> We should rejoice.

3 *Magazines; John Camden Hotten*

These publishers were out of business by the time I reached the West End of London and began to estimate the qualities of various imprints. I put highest in those days the noble firms of Macmillan and Longman, with Blackwood of Edinburgh as a remote but distinguished rival, and John Murray very close at hand. They all published magazines or reviews, or both; and if I name a few of these you will realise what the literary world has lost and is losing by the fact that such periodicals are no longer profitable. There were *Blackwood's, Macmillan's, Longman's, Temple Bar, The Cornhill, The Gentleman's*, in every one of which fiction and essays of the then highest class could appear. It is true that the magazines may already have felt the competition of more popular monthlies such as *The Strand, Pearson's*, and *The Windsor*; but to writers who cared less for money than for the delirium of publication they were, every one of them, beacons of hope. Some were beacons of culture.

The Gentleman's Magazine, founded in 1731 by Edward Cave, had had a succession of learned editors. At this time it was published by Chatto and Windus, the successors of John Camden Hotten; and when I began to work for Chatto and Windus in 1907 I heard many anecdotes of Hotten as what J. M. Dent would have called a "bizair and outré" figure in modern publishing. Edmund Gosse (the not always accurate, who perhaps was seeking to contrast Hotten with Curll) condemned him as "that somewhat notorious tradesman." Andrew Chatto was less severe. But even he, smiling with the kindness of his warm heart, portrayed Hotten as an ambiguous character. Chatto had been Hotten's manager; and when Hotten died suddenly, with his affairs in chaos, Chatto found an artistic partner with money, brought

"The Temple of the Muses": Lackington's Library in Finsbury Square

Puns on Publishers' Names
Georgian and Regency

Frederic Chapman   John Vine Hall

("Chapman·and Hall")

John Bell   John Murray

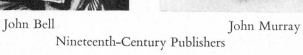

Nineteenth-Century Publishers

his own skill and experience to the task of enlarging, broadening, and stabilising the business, and carried it on under the name with which we are now all so familiar. His offices were at 214 Piccadilly, where a mysterious and still questionable remnant of the Hotten entourage hovered for a time around the newly constituted firm.

Those must have been very queer days indeed; for Hotten published all sorts of semi-historical compilations, some of them containing much out-of-the-way information about Signboards, Social Life in the Reign of Queen Anne, the Clergy, the Stage, the London Parks, the Caricatures of the Georgian Period, etc., printed in diabolically small type and illustrated with diabolical little drawings. He was generally supposed to have written these books himself, with a little aid from hacks; but this cannot have been wholly true. He had some learning, was always short of money, and was an opportunist. Therefore, when the first series of *Poems and Ballads* caused other publishers to tremble for their heads, and Swinburne was furious with them all, Hotten took every risk and was well-rewarded. Swinburne stayed. Theodore Watts-Dunton, his protector but in time his tyrant, continued the association. And Swinburne is still published by Chatto and Windus.

My authority for the following macabre anecdote of Hotten is the late Percy Spalding, who on Andrew Chatto's death became senior partner in the firm. Hotten had published for a number of American authors, from Artemus Ward to Bret Harte; and among these authors was Ambrose Bierce, whose book, *In the Midst of Life*, is a landmark in the history of the American short story. Bierce, like others, had great difficulty in getting any payments from Hotten. He asked for it and waited, asked again, received promises, and had no money. So at last he grew very angry and very threatening, extorted a cheque, and hastily paid it into his bank. The cheque was returned.

Full of rage, Bierce hurried to the office. Hotten was not there. He would take no excuse, but went to Hotten's home, where a woman who answered the door tried to keep him from entering. He brushed aside her protests, forced his way past her, ran up the stairs, and with the dishonoured cheque in his hand entered the publisher's bedroom, shouting. Hotten lay there dead.

4 *Mushroom Publishers; Select Circulating Libraries*

To my mind these stories about William Tinsley and Hotten epitomise the hand-to-mouth ways of many small publishers of the past, especially of the Victorian past. One would not be surprised to find either man in a novel by Dickens, who must have seen similar doings (as I have done) in rickety offices where every shift was used to postpone inevitable bankruptcy.

In such days publishers sold books, if they sold them at all, in hundreds. They might produce perhaps a dozen books in a year, hardly one of which paid its expenses. The publishers had no organisation for the disposal of books; they either allowed heavy discounts to the public (very small ones, of course, to the booksellers, who were starvelings) or they tried to escape the discount evil by publishing at cheeseparing prices. Few had printing works of their own; in this respect Cassells were outstanding and their National Library in weekly volumes at threepence in paper and sixpence in a plain blue cloth binding has never been equalled. Nor had they a force of travellers, or big stock centres in the chief cities, as the modern firms have; but went about the town, and sometimes the country as well, trying to persuade booksellers, drapers, and the like, to take a few copies of the books they wished to circulate. The numbers sold in this way often did not reach a hundred. And if they hoped for success with novels they had to depend entirely on the Select Circulating Libraries.

Select is the key-word. Half way through the eighteenth century the newly established circulating library was far from select. George Colman in 1760 made the heroine's father in his play *Polly Honeycombe* cry out, comparing them to a very corrupt district indeed: "A man might as well turn his daughter loose in Covent Garden as trust the cultivation of her mind to a Circulating Library"; and another writer observed that the books offered by the library were "no better than instruments of debauchery." It may be true that such remarks were made by Puritans, and that the books were less wicked—or would appear to us, who are so much more sophisticated, less wicked—than was assumed. I do not know; my point is only that the Circulating Libraries were not Select.

They became select in an age at which I shall not sneer. But when they became select they became, as all literary authority must do, censorious and dictatorial. One word of complaint from a subscriber sent a book from the shelves of the library, and not yet merely under the counter. And so novels were produced, with prayers for Select Favour, in two or three volumes (if you wish to know with what labour they were sometimes spun out into three volumes you should read George Gissing's *New Grub Street*, which is a heart-cry from the

44

Victorian age) at a guinea-and-a-half apiece; and their nature and prospects of success, according to the less popular and more ambitious French-bred writers, were dictated by the strait-laced:

"We have the villa well in our mind," wrote George Moore. "The father who goes to the city in the morning, the grown-up girls waiting to be married, the big drawing-room where they play waltz music, and talk of dancing-parties. But waltzes will not entirely suffice, nor even tennis; the girls must read. . . . Out of such circumstances the circulating library was hatched.

"The villa made known its want, and art fell on its knees. . . . English fiction became pure, and the garlic and asafoetida with which Byron, Fielding and Ben Jonson so liberally seasoned their works. . . disappeared from our literature."

However, even Moore realised that the circulating libraries, whether select or not, had their function:

"The circulating library lifts the writer out of the precariousness and noise of the wild street of popular fancy into a quiet place where passion is more restrained and there is more reflection. The young and unknown writer is placed at once in a place of comparative security, and he is not forced to employ vile and degrading methods of attracting attention; the known writer, having a certain market for his work, is enabled to think more of it and less of the immediate acclamation of the crowd."

That may have been true of the author; it was true of the publisher only if he could be sure of selling his books to those same libraries. If he were small, and poor, he began to think of nothing but the minimum sale to the libraries. That pre-occupation paralysed him; and if the libraries found the books he published unsuitable for their subscribers he was finished.

5 *J. M. Dent; John Lane; Andrew Chatto; Percy Spalding; Philip Lee Warner; secret classics; T. Fisher Unwin*

I spoke a moment ago as though publishers were all, in those days, bearded. They were not all bearded, of course; I only feel that they must have been a bearded class because those chiefly in my eye in early days wore beards. I never saw the John Murray who was then at the head of that famous business, and I saw the great C. J. Longman only once (if the tall, stately man wearing an iron grey moustache was in fact C. J. Longman); William Heinemann was clean shaven; so was Grant Richards; so was the small, quiet, but irascible Elkin Mathews; and so, I am sure, were other leading men in the trade. But my first book-publishing employer, J. M. Dent; my second, Andrew Chatto; and two other publishers whom I knew by sight, T. Fisher Unwin and John Lane, were all whiskered. Therefore, to me, that was the era of bearded publishers.

Since I want to suggest here how remarkably the progress of publishing has been affected by the idiosyncrasies of individuals I shall begin by speaking of these men, and their era.

Fisher Unwin, having been established for some time at 26 Paternoster Square and 11 Paternoster Buildings, had just moved, at the beginning of the century, to Adelphi Terrace; Lane was in Vigo Street; Chatto at 111 St Martin's Lane; and Dent had taken over the premises vacated by Macmillan at 29 and 30, Bedford Street. I went to these premises in 1901, and from a small box in a corner surveyed the large room, opening directly on to Bedford Street, where the firm's file copies of its publications were kept, and where in winter a lively coal fire welcomed every caller. On the walls of this room hung original drawings by Beardsley—one I loved represented Tannhäuser's return to the Venusberg,—William Hyde, Granville Fell, the brothers Brock, the brothers Robinson, etc. On the floor was a gigantic green cord carpet; and many of the books were bound in green, a fact on which booksellers were in the habit of commenting. When an untried and not very sensible advertising manager took space in *The Daily Mail,* to advertise "Dent's Evergreen Catalogue," the London traveller was so roasted during his first calls that for the rest of the day he sulked in his tent.

There was a locked door at the back of this enormous ground floor, which I presume led up to the premises of the Yorick Club. Upon it, to my unceasing excitement, was a handwritten notice: "No employee is to pass this door" (I think those were the words) and the signature GEORGE LILLIE CRAIK. Craik was a partner in the firm of Macmillan, and husband of the author of *John Halifax, Gentleman.* I knew these things; and although to this day I have never read *John Halifax, Gentleman,* I had been told that it was my father's favourite novel. This notice was still on the door when I left six and a half years later. I do not think anybody else was aware of it.

J. M. Dent was unlike my three previous employers, one of whom was a Scottish gentleman, one a boor, and one an exceedingly gaunt Yankee with a ceremonious manner. Dent was lame, rather under middle height, hobbled very thoughtfully, looked over his spectacles as well as through them, sometimes relapsed into a Yorkshire phrase and accent, and was so silvery that many strangers mistook him for a saint. He had an unusually violent temper, which led him to scream alarmingly at members of his staff and address them, his head thrown back and his beard waggling, as "You donkey!" He never praised; he paid very poorly; he frightened everybody who worked for him; and he one day said wistfully to me (whom he liked), "I don't know how it is; but when we get anybody who is any good he always leaves us."

I have told so many stories of J. M. Dent in my autobiography that I do not like to repeat them, for fear of seeming senile; but I must add that he was a Malaprop, that his spelling was so eccentric that he even had original ways of writing the names of his authors—for example, Arthur Symons was always "Author Simmonds,"—that when annoyed or sorrowful he drew his breath with a horrifying hiss, and that, for two or three years, only I could be trusted to buy his daily lunch, which consisted of a penny roll, a penny pat of butter, a penny piece of cheese, a penny apple, and I think a bottle of ginger beer. I do not remember being afraid of any other man; but I was certainly afraid of J. M. Dent.

He was by trade a binder, and he began publishing because he could not get satisfactory sheets to bind for the gift market. Having had one book printed for himself, he went on to have other books printed; and, almost as it seemed by chance, became a publisher. As a result of his association with Toynbee Hall, he learned that a pocket edition of Shakespeare with reasonably good looks would be a boon. It proved a boon. The Temple Shakespeare, for its day, at a shilling a volume in cloth and eighteenpence in red leather, was perfect. It was followed by the Temple Classics and the Temple Dramatists; by cheap well-produced reprints of Jane Austen, Susan Ferrier, Fielding (Dent drew the line at Smollett, and another firm published a uniform set), Captain Marryat, Walter Savage Landor, Defoe, Sterne, Scott, Dickens, and *The Spectator*; and, of course, the unsurpassed translation of Balzac in forty volumes. Many other reprints were in the Dent list; these reprints, of which Everyman's Library swamped and outdid all the others, hid from common view some extraordinarily venturesome publishing.

The famous Beardsley *Morte D'Arthur*, brought to Dent by that strange, small, ginger man with a bird's chirp and wild eyes, F. H.

Evans, a great pioneer photographer, the friend of Shaw, and the Evans of Jones and Evans, the notable city booksellers, was the most sensational of these ventures. Evans had met Beardsley, then a mere boy; and Dent had been perceptive enough to seize his chance. The association had not continued; Beardsley had moved farther west, to the Bodley Head.

Other Dent efforts, less bold, were bold enough. He published two very early novels by H. G. Wells, *The Wonderful Visit* and *The Wheels of Chance*. He published what I always thought the two most interesting books of Maurice Hewlett, when Hewlett was unknown: *Earthwork out of Tuscany* and *Pan and the Young Shepherd*. He took over from other publishers W. H. Hudson's two early books, *Idle Days in Patagonia* and *A Naturalist in La Plata*; and eventually published a collected Hudson. And he gave employment in the office or on his editorial staff to such men as Gerald Duckworth, A. R. Waller, Edward Hutton, Ernest Rhys, Israel Gollancz (who went to law with him over their agreement and won much money), Philip Lee Warner, Edmund Gardner, and William Macdonald. Macdonald always called Dents "the House of Fang"; but Dent admired and was patient with Macdonald. He had an eye and a nose for good work; he had taste and a real love of books; and if it was true that good men left him as fast as possible, it is also true that they learned and gave much before going. The firm moved from 29 and 30 Bedford Street, after my day, to the fine new premises on the corner of Bedford Street and Chandos Street, where you may now find them.

John Lane's star was setting by the turn of the century; the best impression of his heyday can be gained from Max Beerbohm's *Enoch Soames*, which recaptures that wonderful era of hansom cabs, gas lamps, *The Yellow Book*, and the Café Royal as no other writing has ever done. Mr Beerbohm describes how he met Will Rothenstein, the artist, and continues:

"It was to him I owed my first knowledge of that forever enchanting little world-in-itself, Chelsea, and my first acquaintance with Walter Sickert and other august elders who dwelt there. It was Rothenstein that took me to see, in Cambridge Street, Pimlico, a young man whose drawings were already famous among the few—Aubrey Beardsley, by name. With Rothenstein I paid my first visit to the Bodley Head. By him I was inducted into another haunt of intellect and daring, the domino room of the Café Royal.

"There, on that October evening—there, in that exuberant vista of gilding and crimson velvet set amidst all those opposing mirrors and upholding caryatids, with fumes of tobacco ever rising to the painted and pagan ceiling, and with the hum of presumably cynical conversation broken into so sharply now and again by the clatter of dominoes shuffled on marble tables, I drew a deep breath and 'This indeed,' said I to myself, 'is life.'"

It was life at the end of the nineteenth century; and the Bodley Head, at the sign of which Lane published for Henry Harland, Ernest Dowson, Richard Le Gallienne, Lionel Johnson, "George Egerton," Max himself, John Buchan in his early mystical vein, and the leaders of that elegant band of artists and poets which made *The Yellow Book* seem to carry the Naughty Nineties well up the slopes of Parnassus, was as much the headquarters of life by day as the Café Royal was its headquarters after dark. No matter if grimmer writers were at work elsewhere; here in that deliciously obscure shop in Vigo Street, which can still be seen jutting out as it must have done all those years ago, the aesthetes were kings. As we look back upon them they may seem rather more "period," or dandified, than they intended ever to be; but they were more original than the dandies of nineteen-fifty, who merely copy decadence because they can do nothing else.

Lane was physically a small man. When I knew him his beard was white; he had been described cruelly by an escaped author as resembling "a miniature Silenus"; and I think there was some inequality in his eyes, such as that which Aubrey attributed to Ben Jonson. Arnold Bennett took him the manuscript of a first novel, *A Man from the North*, which he published on the recommendation of his chief "reader," John Buchan; and the association was continued with a slighter work, *Journalism for Women*, recommended by Evelyn Sharp. Bennett did not stay with Lane; and in time, as the nineties faded, the magic of that name, the Bodley Head, grew a little less. It rose when Stephen Phillips took the town with *Paolo and Francesca*, and glittered doubtfully when Lane starred some excellent novels which he had bought outright; but that was towards the end of his life, and later, after gallant work by the subsequent initiator of the Penguin Books, Allen Lane, the business passed into other hands.

The habit of buying copyrights was a feature of novel-publishing at the turn of the century. Chatto and Windus (for I have now reached the third of my bearded publishers, Andrew Chatto) made a practice of it, and although the price varied according to the author, it dropped in the case of unknowns to twenty pounds. Sir Walter Besant, the now neglected historian of London and post-Dickensian author of *All Sorts and Conditions of Men* and *St Catherine's by the Tower*, which were noted in the eighties and nineties, received eight hundred pounds per novel. That represented, for some years, an arrangement satisfactory to both parties; but a time came when Besant began to lose sales, and the firm asked whether, in view of the decline, he would accept a royalty. He refused. Chatto and Windus paid him the eight hundred pounds as usual. And the novel over which this disagreement had arisen was *The Orange Girl*, the greatest success the author ever had.

Besant was dead by the time I went to 111 St Martin's Lane. So was James Payn. Ouida was still alive; and had gone to other publishers. Hall Caine, who had sold three books outright to the firm, had moved to Heinemann. Andrew Chatto still believed himself a master in novel publishing; and according to Arnold Bennett he had a sure answer to any novelist who demurred to his terms for the purchase of a book. The answer was "I have the cheque in my pocket." I never heard Andrew Chatto say this; to me he was a gentle elderly man with a rolling walk, genially sweet in manner to every member of his staff, and much loved. Almost better loved still was his partner, Percy Spalding, who did not pretend to any literary taste, but put his hands in his pockets, jingled his keys and coppers, whistled *Meet me Tonight in Dreamland*, and said to all authors, whatever their pretensions, "Nce, give us a rattling good story!" Some authors, harbingers as it were of modernity and already very scoffing about "story," were amused at the request.

At that time many publishers had their private slogans. Sir Algernon Methuen, who published my own early work, used always to say, in farewell, "Goodbye, my boy; mind and make the next one *human!*" But Percy Spalding's preference for story accompanied an enjoyment of spice; he was very simple, agreeably sentimental, and very generous. It was his habit to give authors royalties beyond their wildest dreams, and when confessing his recklessness he would murmur, "Nce, have to hold a candle to the devil . . . . These men are hard biters, you know!" His almost invisible eyebrows, which he pinched occasionally, to make them grow, danced up and down as he laughed.

Unfortunately, when I went to Chatto and Windus, I found myself in the midst of excitement; for my introduction was made by Philip Lee Warner, a new partner there, whom I had met when he was a

George Bernard Shaw

H. G. Wells

Lytton Strachey

Modern Publisher and Author

reader for Dents. Lee Warner was a flying figure; very tall, with sweeping coat-tails, blinking eyes, and a fantastic mock-snarling humour. He stirred the firm from sluggishness by his energy; but he terrified the other partners, who breathed more freely at his departure at the end of a three years' probationary period. He represented the great leap of the firm into colour books about other countries and cities (also the first Medici Prints), and I learned for the first time how a book as written by the author may be merely the first draft of the book as published after ferocious revision by the publisher.

This responsibility of the publisher for the book has grown in the last fifty years with, as it seems to me, the higher educational attainments of modern publishers. Many best-sellers of the half-century have been rewritten in publishers' offices or by their authors in response to publishers' recommendations. Not only did Lee Warner rewrite books very copiously; he passed them to me to rewrite. I should not like to tell you what authors I set my prentice hand to in this way; but I must declare that some of them afterwards expressed gratitude, and all of them modestly accepted the revisions. Two at least were quite proud of their remodelled books as rewritten, and were able to receive compliments on their excellence with complacency.

Lee Warner left the firm; and, to my astonishment, I was asked to stay and act as reader. In the end this arrangement answered well; and as I became an author myself I met other authors who brought their books to Chatto and Windus. In this way the "character" of the list changed once again. It had been based on three-volume novels, with Swinburne and Stevenson as strange brilliances from afar. It was then, after a period of decline, rushed into art, translated memoirs, medieval history, and illustrated topography under Lee Warner's guidance. When Geoffrey Whitworth and I took charge it sobered, touched modernity, became rather eccentrically selective in its fiction and verse, and had successes ranging from Lytton Strachey and Aldous Huxley to *The Young Visiters*. These in turn prepared the way for the firm today.

If I have seemed to dwell too long here and previously on individual publishers, it is because I am writing, not history, but a personal impression of the bookman's London. What I have said will show the fortunes and changes in any publishing business of more than ten years' standing. Publishers tire, as other men tire. In my time I have seen them, also, continuing too long—obstinately—on a course which in the preceding decade has been full of a contemporary briskness.

They have lost flexibility, ideas, and authors. They have not died, because in the past they have combined adventurousness with a sense of what is called "the back list." Now the back list is composed of books which go on selling, year after year, without advertisement, sometimes in thousands, sometimes in hundreds, sometimes only in scores. These books sell for the reason that readers of various types discover them almost by accident and seek to possess them almost by force. You and I may never hear their titles; but they are in fact classics, classics in some cases without reputation. I do not mean what is sometimes called "the schoolgirl's bible," *Maria Monk*; nor *Little Black Sambo*, which has immense prestige in the nursery. I mean such works as Whiston's *Josephus*, Cobbett's *Grammar*, and hundreds of medical and technological books, anthologies, and aids to the unschooled. Most new books are dead in three months—cynics say they are born dead;—but these live indefinitely, or would have done so if Goering had not sent fire-bombers over London which in a night destroyed stocks and stereos, and brought that happy flow of sale to a distressing end.

I imagine that Fisher Unwin must have published large numbers of such classics. He is the fourth and last of my beards, the largest and bulkiest of them all, and in some respects the ablest. He was well served by his readers, the most notable of whom was Edward Garnett, the discoverer while he read for Unwin of the novels of Joseph Conrad and W. H. Hudson; but in himself he had more mind than Dent or Chatto, though less taste than Dent and Lane. Like several other publishers of his generation he was a Liberal; and as the husband of a daughter of Richard Cobden he published John Morley's dreary life of that great if not especially amusing man. His interests must have been wide; he was a member of the Johnson Society as well as the Reform Club; and he had dignity. He needed this dignity; for his costume was unusual. He wore a grey, tailed morning suit; and upon his large, imposing head he carried an elderly straw boater.

Unwin was not, in his own office, a beloved figure; and by authors he was thought stingy. Nevertheless he had courage in publishing, and when other men were shy of Wells's *Ann Veronica* he bought it without fear. He also, in the little series called the Pseudonym Library, introduced several writers of fiction who were found very advanced for their years. He published John Oliver Hobbes; the early tales of "Benjamin Swift" (William Romaine Paterson); one or two books by George Moore; and, much to his credit, both the First Novel

Library, which gave beginners, less pampered then than now, a label and a start, and the original Mermaid Series of old plays. The First Novel Library's greatest success was *The Way of an Eagle*, by Ethel M. Dell; the Mermaid Series is still unchallenged.

As you will have noticed, Unwin's publications were miscellaneous. While he often published good books one could not take it for granted that everything he published had character. Too often it was as tedious as the style in which it was produced, taste in production not being Unwin's strong point. He also had a habit of publishing, remaindering, and re-publishing books in successively cheaper editions, which was disconcerting to book-lovers. The habit effectively assured every book of its ultimate reader; and my disapproval of it is not ethical but aesthetic.

At first, as I have said, Unwin's business was carried on in Paternoster Square or Paternoster Buildings; but he followed the westward movement and settled until the end of his active career in Adelphi Terrace, near the old Savage Club and not half a minute from the flats of Bernard Shaw at No. 10 and J. M. Barrie at Adelphi Terrace House. I cannot picture him as the friend of these or any other authors. One day, immensely conscious of his own dignity, he came and sat near to Arnold Bennett and myself at the Reform Club. I murmured to Bennett: "Do you see who's at the next table?" Bennett replied, with brief humour: "I do. The . . . Enemy of Man."

6 *Macmillan; William Heinemann; Algernon Methuen; literary agents; Grant Richards; Martin Secker; a revival in the Novel*

In my opinion Fisher Unwin was not only the last of the bearded publishers of his era; he represents the end of a publishing type. Whereas the greater publishers of the nineteenth century all responded actively to a broadening of scientific and social horizons, the lesser men, while acknowledging what was thought to be indefeasible progress, could not rival the greater houses in consistency of standard. You have only to read Mr Charles Morgan's book on *The House of Macmillan* to see what a snowball success quality can produce, and with what leisure and dignity a Victorian publisher could so build a list that the popular—Charlotte Yonge, Rosa Nouchette Carey, and Mrs Henry Wood—could be combined with the seriously instructive, from Charles Kingsley and J. R. Green to John Morley, Alfred Marshall, and Sir James Frazer, Hardy, Kipling, "Elizabeth", and Hewlett, without loss of prestige. Lesser firms than Macmillan were dependent on the luck of a morning's postal delivery. They could not plan on the grand scale; and their publications in one sense were haphazard and lacking in authority. The great scholars were already committed; the snobs, seeking *cachet*, went where it was bred.

However, just when stability and the Victorian age seemed likely —outside Vigo Street—to continue for ever, publishing took a new turn. Men with fresh and vigorous ideas sought the trade. They did not want to be inferior Macmillans; they believed Bodley Head authors to need weeding; and they had great ambitions.

The first of these men, and in my opinion the most important of them all, set up business on the west side of Bedford Street, Covent Garden, at No. 21. His name was William Heinemann. Heinemann has never been surpassed in the trade for brilliance of taste, daring, and success. Being a German Jew, he brought to English publishing an altogether new sense of Continental life and Continental literature. This led him, with the active cooperation of Edmund Gosse and others, to establish a series of novels by international authors, to produce Mrs Garnett's complete Turgenev and some less famous translations of a complete Björnson. Archer's Ibsen was revised and completed (the prose dramas had previously been published by an undeservedly forgotten publisher named Walter Scott); and by 1912 Mrs Garnett's complete Dostoevsky was begun. For some reason Heinemann refused the Garnett translation of Chekhov, which I persuaded Chatto and Windus to undertake; but this was the only lapse in a sequence of bold assaults intended to rouse the English mind from its three-volume stodginess.

Nor was Heinemann solely concerned with foreign books. It was he who published Whistler's *Gentle Art of Making Enemies*. He had Henry James in James's thrillingly effective middle period, and some of the best of Conrad. He captured other writers of several generations, from H. G. Wells, Israel Zangwill, Max Beerbohm, Somerset Maugham, E. F. Benson, and Hall Caine in the nineties to Henry Handel Richardson in the new century and D. H. Lawrence, Gilbert Cannan, and other youngsters in the next decade. He published Pinero's plays. And he could surprise immense popularity with Sarah Grand, "Richard Dehan" (Clo Graves), and William de Morgan, the septuagenarian beginner. Whatever he did, he did with an air. The Nicholson windmill on his title-pages gave every book a look of quality;

it was a stamp, a hall mark. The publisher of that book, it said, had verve and decision; taste, judgment, and a policy. He was the publisher without a beard.

In person Heinemann was plumply not above middle height, with a round pale face and a rather resentful mouth which seemed made for bitter retorts. He wrote poetic tragedies which John Lane published for him, was rude, ruthless, impulsive, and brimming with nervous energy. And in a few years he had established a name and an organisation which left other publishers envious. Andrew Chatto, striking at his own knee, said "Heinemann? By comparison with me Heinemann is up to there!" One does not speak thus of a rival unless his shadow is that of a giant.

I think it was not Heinemann but Algernon Methuen who first took the public into his confidence by advertising the number of editions a book had achieved before and immediately after publication. Methuen began his success by publishing a brief, innocuous tale by Edna Lyall called *Derrick Vaughan, Novelist*, which came out at the end of the eighteen eighties; by nineteen hundred he was the largest publisher of novels (until George Hutchinson, with even more extensive methods of mass salesmanship, bore away that particular palm) in existence.

He advertised most of the romantics en masse—Marie Corelli, Anthony Hope, Gilbert Parker, Robert Hichens, W. B. Maxwell, and, in a heyday of immense reputation, Eden Phillpotts;—and said, not how many copies of a book had been printed, but how many editions or impressions. The public did not question the competence of those who gave the printing-orders; but jumped with excitement at learning that as many as three or four or seventeen editions had been required before or immediately after publication. At the beginning of a season Methuen announced in bulk twenty or thirty novels and a score or more of books which were not fiction. He gave, two or three months in advance, the exact dates of publication. And the names of his authors promised a delight which would nowadays be scorned as "escape," but which in those more tranquil hours was considered to be merely a widening of horizons. All sedateness departed from publishers' advertising. For a time, between the last Boer War and the First World War, the trade almost ceased to be in a parlous state.

We learned that Methuen could sell books. He was at the same time in the market to pay what were said to be large sums of money to authors on account of earnings from royalties. No longer were novels to be sold outright to publishers; no longer were royalties to be gradually and very painfully earned; the author was to enjoy at once the fruits of his labour and popularity. He was to be bid for as if he were a precious antique at auction. Heinemann might not be cordial towards those new menaces to publishers who were called literary agents; but Methuen, accepting them, turned them to his own account.

Literary agents? I have forgotten to tell you that these intermediaries had arrived in the book world. Perhaps they killed the old-style publisher—the "demi-bookseller" of Roger North's diatribe—who paid neither advance nor royalty. He muddled his accounts, cheated his clients, and succumbed to bankruptcy when he could hold out no longer. At any rate, they and Walter Besant's Society of Authors, which was gathering members and power, did this. And a publisher, such as Methuen, who invented new series and persuaded brisk new men to write the books for these series, who could and did sell a hundred thousand copies of a novel by Marie Corelli and many thousands of the celebrated *Garden of Allah*, by Robert Hichens (which had so many impressions that one pictured printers putting it back on the machines as fast as they took it off), could hold his own with any literary agent in England.

What did the agent do? He said, "You must pay a royalty on every copy of the book. And, on the day of publication, you must pay me, as the author's representative, much money, perhaps more than you think the total royalties will ever reach, for the privilege of publishing this and two or three more of his books." If you object that this made the author a very expensive person to the publisher, and his work a very commercial article indeed, you will find many publishers agreeing with you. But, as to the commerce of letters, Dryden contracted with Tonson to deliver so many thousand verses for so many guineas, which seems a fairly commercial arrangement to make for immortal poetry; and, as for expensiveness, so (subsequently) successful an author as Arnold Bennett employed an agent because he personally was incapable of driving a hard bargain with publishers.

This is not the common report. Bennett made on his first novel enough to buy himself a new hat. His early "fantasias" were sold outright to a newspaper syndicate for seventy-five pounds apiece. It was not until *The Old Wives' Tale*, with a comparatively small circulation, made his reputation in 1908 that a tremendous rumour ran round London. Arnold Bennett, we were told, had agreed with Methuen to accept eight hundred pounds in advance of royalties on each of three novels. It had all been managed by an agent; and Methuen was going to burn his fingers. You will not be surprised to learn that the amount was exaggerated; Methuen offered, in fact, advances of £300, £350, and £400 on the three books, which were *Clayhanger*, *Hilda Lessways*, and *These Twain*. He did not burn his fingers. Nor did Bennett grow wealthy on these books.

Methuen was not a finger-burner. He was a shrewd, financially-careful man who combined scholarship with strong business instinct. He made and kept a great deal of money; something like a quarter of a million pounds. His list never had the fiery boldness and originality of Heinemann's list; it was produced well for its period, but in a stand-ardised form which gave learned books no dignity; and in all other respects, especially those of publicity, it was extremely efficient. Methuen's educational experience greatly helped him; he read many of the books he published, and believed in his own taste; and in what are called *belles lettres* and anecdotal topography he owed much to his literary adviser E. V. Lucas. He thus helped to carry publishing on-wards towards its present state, parlous or otherwise.

Nevertheless I think he was timid. When the First World War began he assumed that books would stop selling and that it would be over in six months. He therefore invited writers such as myself to abandon authorship until the world was stable again; and he suggested to authors of renown that they should accept a fifty per cent. cut in their advances. No doubt his mood changed as the war continued;. he had ceased, all the same, to pioneer and had begun to think of safety.

One who thought too little of safety all his life was the first of my remaining publishers—the men who, in my opinion, have brought modernity into the trade and marked it with their own personalities. This was Grant Richards. Richards was first employed by Simpkin, Marshall, the big wholesale booksellers of Paternoster Row, who had their premises and whole tremendous stock destroyed in a single night by fire-bombers, and who are now re-formed into what is virtually a distributive centre for the more practical of contemporary publishers. Richards had gathered much experience from the old-style Simpkins.

He established himself at No 9 Henrietta Street, Covent Garden (Duckworth's is No. 3), started the World's Classics in a series of fat, dumpy volumes which looked splendid value for a shilling, moved to 48 Leicester Square, published Bernard Shaw and Shaw's master, Samuel Butler, had a remarkable arrangement with A. E. Housman whereby he paid no royalty on *A Shropshire Lad* for as long as he kept it in print at sixpence, and was the first English publisher to take a large space in a daily newspaper to advertise a single book. Also the first to use short, chatty advertisements.

I will not say that the large spaces have been a blessing to publishers; but they drew attention to Richards as nothing else could have done. His advertising, the Dumpy Books for Children, the dumpy World's Classics, the fact that he published his own novels, of which at least *Caviare* had the appearance of success, and an almost reckless air of being always at the height of youth and spirits, made him for a time resemble a comet. Much that he published was flashy—for example, *The Unspeakable Scot*, an attack on a whole people by T. W. H. Crosland, who read for him;—and the recklessness which observers read into his doings had its inevitable results. A publisher more than once bankrupt loses his authors and his credit.

If Richards could have restrained his impulse to gamble, and if he had never stood up, he would have been a fine publisher and an impressive man. He was very handsome, and his monocled profile was distinguished. But when he rose, owing to the fact that his legs were too short for his splendid torso, he lost dignity. When circumstances allowed, he was a generous and disinterested man. And he gave bright colour to publishing.

Less flamboyant than Richards, and of a younger generation, Martin Secker was equally adventurous but much quieter and wiser. Secker, when reading for Eveleigh Nash in the year 1909, recommended publication of a romance of the eighteenth century by a new writer named Mackenzie. It was called *The Passionate Elopement*, and was written with a grace recalling to Secker the finesse of his favourite nineties. The recommendation was over-ruled by another reader, and *The Passionate Elopement* was rejected. But Secker soon afterwards came into possession of a thousand pounds, on which he ventured into publishing on his own account. He immediately, therefore, wrote to Compton Mackenzie, asking if *The Passionate Elopement* had been sold. It had not been sold. Upon that book was based the success of the new business.

Here distinctive production and again distinctive advertising of a single book drew attention to the new publisher. Even more important was the fact that Secker, knowing exactly what authors he wanted to publish, published hardly any other authors at all. He had a plan for a series of short monographs on modern writers; and he was justified in his plan by the quality of the first books in the series, those on Wilde, by Arthur Ransome, and Hardy, by Lascelles Abercrombie. Also he was helped by the fact that the years following the accession and death of King Edward VII saw a curious burgeoning of the English novel.

The picturesque had been killed by the Boer War; Kipling was temporarily in eclipse; art (as represented by Henry James) and back-street realism had made their surprises and were no longer surprises. But we had Joseph Conrad, whose *Lord Jim*, in 1900, was just Victorian, and whose *Nostromo* was published in 1904; H. G. Wells, who had done with romantic prophecy and who was making a new assault with *Kipps* in 1906 and *Tono-Bungay* in 1909; John Galsworthy, also documenting society with *The Man of Property* in 1906; and Arnold Bennett, bringing the Midlands to town in *The Old Wives' Tale* in 1908. These men represented the older generation. Conrad was in his fifties; the three others had been born ten years later, in 1866 or 1867.

By 1910, also, a younger generation, the members of which had been born between 1882 and 1885, was becoming active. Secker had Mackenzie. He wanted, and gained, Gilbert Cannan, who had published his first three books, *Peter Homunculus*, *Devious Ways*, and *Little Brother*, with Heinemann and who wished to change his publisher. He either wanted, or was sought by, Hugh Walpole, whose third novel, about schoolmasters, *Mr Perrin and Mr Traill*, had made a stir in the list of Mills and Boon. And so there were three of the young reputations; and their common association with a fine, dashing publisher was truly helpful to literary commentators. These found, in spite of the fact that the three young novelists were all different, that a new school in fiction had arisen. It was the Secker school.

One saw Secker novels on drawing-room tables in good society; and each one of them was recognisably a Secker novel. One read, in the literary and political weeklies, which in 1912 or so had plenty of space for criticism, long reviews of the literary monographs. And one knew, or thought one knew, if one were on the inside of the literary world, that Secker published only what he personally admired. At a bound his reputation for quality was established; and it was a reputation associated in people's minds with youth. For the first time there arose in literary history the dogma that youth is a virtue; it glittered as a special phenomenon of the twentieth century.

The 1914–18 war, which by old men was called "a young men's

war" (and by young men "an old men's war"), emphasised the division of men and women into young and old; but Secker had started the movement by publishing three young men of great promise. If he had also at this time published D. H. Lawrence, as he was to do later, he would have swept the field and monopolised the attention of the critical press.

And yet in many respects Secker remained as conservative as a man could be. Conducting his business from two rooms and a basement at "No. 5 John Street" in the Adelphi (this was a further identification, owing to the earlier fame of a novel by Richard Whiteing bearing that title), he refused to have the telephone installed in his office; he had no secretary; and, besides demonstrating his knowledge that a letter left unanswered for a fortnight answers itself, he wrote to authors by hand or in his own typing. The outside world might hardly have existed for him. The one adventure was publishing; the two literary periods in which he was interested were the nineties and the nineteen-tens. Even as regards the latter he was highly selective, because long after I had lent him an admired novel by a distinguished contemporary he mildly asked me "What was the name of that very good book I couldn't read?"

To my mind, Secker's attitude towards publishing was the nearest thing possible in modern times to the attitude of Tonson, Dodsley, Pickering, and the second John Murray. It was personal and self-disciplined. The vulgarity which caused other houses to covet size and great sales, to say "if we don't publish it somebody else will," and to lose in a jumble of chance pickings all appearance of a criterion, was countered by distinguished eclecticism. There have been greater publishers, less romantic publishers than Secker; there has never been one who more steadfastly respected his own judgment and with no presumption at all acted upon it.

7 Jonathan Cape; Stanley Unwin; Victor Gollancz; Bloomsbury

Looking around, as I approach the present day, I see young firms and old-established firms with new direction making history. But I shall refer to only two other publishers for their obvious influence upon our age, and to three others for a greater, if less generally appreciated, influence upon the organisation of the trade.

First, then, comes Jonathan Cape, once a traveller for the house of Duckworth; then for a time with the Medici Society, where Philip

Lee Warner darted and dared in middle-age as he had done in youth; and finally, in partnership with Wren Howard, and with the majestic assistance of the best "editor" or "reader" who ever lived, Edward Garnett, a publisher. By starting at 30 Bedford Square Cape set a fashion among publishers. He was not the first to go there, for Stanley Unwin, after buying the business of George Allen, with premises in Charing Cross Road, established his new firm, George Allen and Unwin, at 40 Museum Street as long ago as 1914. But residence is one thing and fashion another. Cape set the fashion.

He set fashions in other ways as well; for his firm introduced a new, severe, and very elegant style of book-production which was maintained through the Second World War at a time when some other houses, announcing "complete conformity with the authorised economy standards," made books look like remainder biscuits. He has also been noted for nursing until they grew famous good authors who at first missed their mark. But his chief distinction is that although he has never been among the publishers to whom solemn biographers and historians first thought of taking their books he has so rarely published the less than good that his imprint is of great value.

Finally, Victor Gollancz, once at the Cambridge University Press, later manager of Sir Ernest Benn's book business, and a publisher on his own account since 1928, has had three great influences upon modern publishing. He introduced the unmistakably uniform yellow paper dustcover; he took enormous spaces in the Sunday newspapers to advertise single books (on a scale unapproached by Richards or Secker); and by his confident advocacy of the books he published carried them to unprecedented sales, of which he gave the figures in astounding thousands. Starting in Henrietta Street, Covent Garden, he has remained true to his home; he has proclaimed his Left Wing politics and revived the polemical pamphlet; and he has rattled all older publishers, and some newer ones, by his high-pressure publishing. But he has always walked alone. He is quite outside the contemporary movement towards publishers' cooperation, led by Stanley Unwin, Geoffrey Faber, and George Harrap. If this rationalising movement succeeds, Stanley Unwin and his colleagues (but especially Stanley Unwin) will have achieved a triumph over the trade's hitherto invincible individualism.

How far such schemes are from the kind of publishing I first knew! Then, at the beginning of the century, every publisher's office was his castle, where he sat in mighty solitude waiting for the trade to come to him, and where—however parlous the state of publishing—his bills were comparatively small, his pace unpressed, and his financial ambitions modest. I liked those days. I was young in them. A book was still "the precious life-blood of a master spirit" and its advent a thrilling promise of delight. I remember when the publication of that wearisome biography of Gladstone by John Morley was the sensation of a year; when Kipling's *Kim*, Maurice Hewlett's *The Forest Lovers*; Hardy's *The Dynasts*, and any new play by Shaw or Granville Barker, any new book by Wells or Chesterton or Belloc or Arnold Bennett was something for which we who were young ran swiftly. I no longer run swiftly; the mass production and absorption of stunt books seems to me to have reduced current literature to a chatter.

Meanwhile the publishers have moved to Bloomsbury, and plan and prosper in the shadow of the British Museum. I have spoken of Allen and Unwin, in Museum Street, and Cape in Bedford Square; there are Doubledays, Heinemanns, and my friend Hamish Hamilton in Great Russell Street; the new Bodley Head in Little Russell Street; Faber and Faber in Bedford Square; Harrap in High Holborn; Michael Joseph in Bloomsbury Street; Hammond, Hammond in Gower Street; Dakers in Store Street; and the Cresset Press in Fitzroy Square. Others lie within five minutes' walk. It is a formidable array.

You can stroll about the district, looking at the dignified old houses and finding every now and again, beside a broad Regency door, a small brass plate telling of the unseen activity within. You can imagine yourself back in the past, when no such plates marked these houses, and when horse carriages stood outside them and hansom cabs whirled round the corners with the kind of sound never heard in London in these days except on the Radio, where they are produced by "effects." You will possibly allow yourself a little emotion.

Very few London publishers, however, can rival their New York brothers in the matter of space; and when you enter the premises of most of them there will be the same mixture of the high calling and the dismal litter of unsold, unpacked books; the bales of stock, the letters, contracts, drawings, samples, typewriters, men with trolleys, booksellers' collectors, and other odds and ends which have always been there and always will be there. If there is a waiting-room for visitors, it will certainly be the size of a cupboard, and you may have to sit against a packing-case.

I was once thrown into a publishers' waiting-room which had been used for years by a sandwich-eating member of the staff—or perhaps some hungry regular visitor of the eighteen-fifties. No principal had ever entered it. I know of only one publishers' waiting-room which, as one uses the term in general conversation, can be called a room. In the others, as an old hand, I appreciatively sniff the mouldering air, and look about me at the rubbish as if I lived again in the last days of Queen Victoria.

How those days come back to me as I write! I see them, I hear them, I smell them. The world is full of bearded publishers, one of whom, perhaps, will publish my first book! As in a kaleidoscope I view the changes of the publishing trade in fifty years. Changes? There are no changes; all is as it was in nineteen hundred and one.

IV

London Booksellers

1 *Ordering a book; booksellers' "collectors"; "answering";
Subscription dinners*

There was once a play called *My
Lady's Dress*. It was not a very good play, because it was one of those
deliberately planned affairs which owe nothing to the imagination;
but, bating this, it held a germ of meaningful discussion. That is to
say, the play pictured what I seem to remember as the progress of a
wedding dress from the order and designing of it, through the work-
rooms in which its various parts were made and stitched together, to
the wearing or non-wearing of it on the nuptial day. The lesson was
painfully obvious from the beginning.

I refer to this play because when you and I order a book from the
bookseller it does not occur to us to consider how the book was written
and printed and published, nor how, from the moment of our ordering,
the copy we eventually receive (or, at this day, do not receive) is
obtained. In present circumstances it is not obtained; it is what is called
"answered." An hour spent invisibly at a publisher's trade counter
would be instructive to the occasional book-buyer.

In former days I used to slip into the trade department at Dents or
Chattos and hear the peculiar hoarse chant—like that, I presume, of
galley-slaves—of men reading over long lists of titles, apparently in
the hope that some one of these titles would quicken into sympathy
the cynical and indifferent publisher's assistant on the other side of the
counter. This assistant, secure in his job and knowledge, might be
examining his finger-nails or looking into space or chatting with a
friend; the chanting man, whose pronunciation of difficult names
showed despairing ingenuity, would peer over the top of his leather-
reinforced notebook, once more examine the scrawls written there,
and continue until he reached the end of them. Sometimes the assistant
would interject a mysterious word, or the name of another publisher,
or the phrase—if the collector's pause had been insistently prolonged—
"Not ahrs."

I used to see the chanters, who were booksellers' runners or collectors, trudging along the streets with great canvas sacks over their

64

shoulders and those stout notebooks in their calloused hands. They were always miserable. They went from publisher to publisher, in all weathers, and flung their sacks on the counter as a preliminary to the act of thumbing through their notebooks. Then, pencil stubs poised, they would take down a price, make a horizontal mark through a title, and continue the dreary chant. Sometimes one of them received what he wanted, which was one or half a dozen volumes; and then the assistant would write in a carbon-sheeted invoice book and the collector would sign his name on the invoice, where the assistant would read it upside down. Then the sack would again be slung across the bludgeoned shoulder and the collector would depart.

Collectors still circulate from publisher to publisher. Their lot is still hard, because publishers usually cannot supply the books that are asked for. The assistant gives a vague reply—it is called an "answer," because every book nowadays has to be "answered"—and the answer is usually "R.P. No date," which means that what is wanted is being reprinted and the date of publication of the reprint is not yet known. The book in fact is not being reprinted; but, as the person on whose behalf the bookseller is demanding this title may be its author, assistants have to be circumspect. The author, if he hears that his work is out of print, will inevitably assail the publisher, either in person or by letter or through his agent, in a fine fury of indignation. And as the publisher is unable to reprint, but at the same time does not wish this particular book to be lost to him for ever, every answer given to a collector is diplomatic—which is to say indefinite and discouraging. In actual diplomacy such an answer would be described as one which "does not close the door." It really means that the book is out of print until the next blue moon.

Having received his "answer," the collector removes himself, no longer flinging the sack over his shoulder as in the past, but wrapping it round such books as he has obtained on his tour, and putting the resulting bundle under his arm. I suppose this is less exhausting, or less servile, than the old "coalman" action. The collector looks more prosperous than of old; he is more intelligent. His chant is no hopeless croak; and he may once have read a few books, which his predecessor obviously had never done.

In case you think, however, that the bookseller's lot in olden times was altogether cheerless, and that every publisher treated him as an open enemy, let me record an ancient practice in the book world, which began, or was in existence, in the eighteenth century (when, however, booksellers cooperated in publishing), and continued until at least the eighteen-eighties. This was the Subscription Dinner. Instead of being waited on by publishers' representatives, or travellers, the principal booksellers were bidden to a semi-yearly feast. The grand old bearded publishers presided at the feast, full of courteous bonhomie; while lesser members of their staffs mixed freely with the visitors and encouraged them to feel safe. After dinner, when all had eaten and drunk with delight, the bearded men brought forth lists of their forthcoming publications, and received what I feel sure must have been bumper orders.

I am sorry this old practice has died out. One pictures the feasts as survivals of the Dickensian past. They may have resulted in morning regrets, even bankruptcy; but it is heart-warming to think of publishers and booksellers getting cosily together. Though they do this nowadays at annual conventions, sales are not discussed at annual conventions. It is still usual when such junketings are over, and travellers call to announce new publications, for booksellers gloomily to indicate the unsold books on their shelves and suggest that something should be done about those before new purchases are made.

2 *How booksellers began; Charles Young; Frederick H. Evans; John Wilson and others*

I wish to speak here of the changes whereby those who in the seventeenth and eighteenth centuries were printers and booksellers became in the nineteenth century publishers only; while a new class of men, who neither printed nor published, took over the name and as I believe unrewarding occupation of "bookseller." At some time after that great act of cooperation, the set of English Poets for which Johnson wrote his *Lives*, the word "publisher" began to distinguish a hierarchy.

One thinks at once of the ever increasing prestige of publishers such as Murray, Longman, Bentley, and Macmillan; and grows curious to know where the new class, which was that of men who were booksellers only, came from. My suggestion is that they may have developed from the circulating libraries. These libraries, established about the middle of the eighteenth century, lent all the new novels which were so eagerly read by Jane Austen, her sister, and her heroines, Mary Russell Mitford and her correspondents, and the unidentified patrons of Mrs Opie, Mrs Inchbald, Miss Ferrier, and Mrs Brunton; but unless

66

these novels were published, as Miss Burney's later works were published, by subscription, the libraries presumably sold as well as lent them. And, if that is so, may not the booksellers who have now been forced to establish libraries at the backs of their bookselling shops be reversing an ancient practice?

When books grew very cheap indeed at the end of the nineteenth century, when the Hundred Best were named by Sir John Lubbock, and when Dumas, Fenimore Cooper, and the Scotts, Walter and Michael, in red cloth bindings were spawned for fourpence-three-farthings a time on happy youth, they were sidelines for drapers, just as one still sees the cheapest books of all in newsagents' and sweet-stuff shops. But the general position of inferiority had been established. The bookseller was doomed to be the middle-man. Fifty years ago, what with iniquitously small discounts from the publishers and idiotic discounts to the public, those who led the London trade might receive twopence in the shilling and an extra copy in the dozen books; but when J. M. Dent used the term "those reskels" we all knew that he spoke of a depressed class.

These shambling, hoarse-voiced collectors were a sign. They were sent out daily upon a graceless quest; and they returned every afternoon to shops where unsold books which had never had any protection but flimsy tissue or glassine covers grew increasingly battered. Booksellers' assistants were always shabby and disheartened; sales were very small; and while some men had customers who valued first-hand advice, and were in the finest tradition of bookselling, it was too often the case that potential customers turned quickly away from tiny, jumbled shops in which every possible answer was dusty.

The good men were exceptional. There was Charles Young, of the Kensington firm of Lamley's. He was small, intelligent, and a book-lover; in young manhood the friend of Arnold Bennett and "George Bourne" (the brother of a Farnham bookseller named Sturt); and publisher of Bennett's *Polite Farces* and other minor uncommercial books. In days of less vociferous competition he would have been a Tonson or a Davies; but he was content with meagre rewards, and missed the distinction he might have attained. There was Frank Denny, who died not long ago, and who for many years bravely kept the Strand from being bookless. He was quiet and friendly to a friend, a great music-lover with a sweet, minute, caressing voice. But on the subject of publishers, and sometimes of authors, he was always sarcastically amusing, and could be terrible in scorn. There was the butler-like

67

but learned Arthur Humphreys, of Hatchards, in Piccadilly, who had immense bibliographical knowledge and was a good bookseller greatly relied on by the nobility and gentry. And, finally, there was the firm of Jones and Evans, in Queen Street, Cheapside.

This shop, on the east side of the street, was a haunt of writers. At a time when the City was still cultured, it attracted all who distinguished between books and boxes of chocolates; and that was because it was run by some of the best British booksellers of modern times. First came Frederick H. Evans, whom I have mentioned earlier as the friend of Shaw, a photographer well in advance of his period, and an early discoverer of Aubrey Beardsley. Evans was a small, eager man who, although not in the book trade for many years, gave the Jones and Evans business its standing. He was not the only one to do so. There came to Queen Street two other partners: William Whittaker, a big, bald, ponderous man who once tried to discourage me from having anything to do with books, which he said were doomed, and John Wilson, who is still with us and is cordially known to every bookman in London.

Wilson came here from Glasgow in 1910. At that time he took an active interest in publishing; and spent two profitable years in the house of Constable. But he then realised that he was at heart a bookseller, and he went to Jones and Evans. There, just before the First World War, young poets such as Rupert Brooke, Lascelles Abercrombie, and John Drinkwater; Walter Emanuel of *Punch*; A. B. Walkley, the *Times* dramatic critic; and many more made a practice of visiting the shop, talking, learning, and filling it with happiness. Such gatherings of talent were the nearest thing this century has known to the gatherings of authors over books in the eighteenth century.

With the war the literary scene changed. Wilson himself was away from books for three and a half years. And shortly after his return he, too, moved west, to the shop—at that time on the north side of Oxford Street—of J. and E. Bumpus. Here, with for the first and only time plenty of space at his disposal, he was able to do great work for books, by means of exhibitions similar in scope and enterprise to those now undertaken by the National Book League. Alas! circumstances changed again; and Bumpuses had to move to their present premises on the left side of Oxford Street as you go to the Marble Arch. Authors, publishers, librarians, bibliophiles, brain-pickers, neophytes, and ordinary people such as you and I go to Wilson for advice. He is never too busy for anybody or anything. And he has triumphed over every obstacle to bookselling.

Wilson is a good name in the bookselling trade; for Hubert Wilson, who carries on the business of Alfred Wilson of Gracechurch Street, in the City, is another man of exceptional drive. He not only sells books, and courageously recommends those he admires ; he also does his utmost to bring booksellers together, to teach them to use their brains, even, it seems to me, to lend them some of his own brains. Under a pseudonym he used to contribute vigorous articles—they shook the trade; I almost said they shook the world—to *The Bookseller*. And he and another man, Frank Ward of Baker Street, brought such modern ideas to London bookselling that with a few more (including John Wilson) they gave it a new, serious outlook.

In speaking of these individuals, who are associated with their own shops, I may have seemed to forget the great book-centres of W. H. Smith and Son and the magnificent book departments to be found in the big stores, such as Harrods. I had not forgotten them; they are splendidly organised for the public service. But each centre, each book department, for all its importance, is no more than a detail in the larger scheme of noble enterprises. It is extraordinarily efficient; throughout the country there are small booksellers who owe nearly every one of their virtues to the wholesale activity of Harrods or Smiths. Forgive me if I do no more than indicate great splendours. I must quickly pass to another branch of the trade in which, as it seems to me, individuals become kings by their own unaided efforts; men who no longer struggle to sell books that nobody wants but who by commanding realms of gold command likewise keys to the millennium. I need not explain that I mean those who sell secondhand books.

3 *From Paternoster Row to Charing Cross Road*

Paternoster Row, Holywell Street, Farringdon Road. The first and second of these are gone; the third seems to have shrunk; but out of old circumstance has grown the crowded marvel of Charing Cross Road, of Great Russell Street and its tributaries, the grandeurs of Quaritch in Grafton Street, Thorp in Albemarle Street, Sotheran in Sackville Street, Pickering and Chatto in King Street, St James's; all of them signs of wealth and health. A man may decide to offer a few old books, bought for a few shillings at a local sale or taken from his own shelves. He may sell them, if they are cheap novels, at a profit of a half-crown. And from this experiment he may move like a comet gathering a tail of dust—gold dust, let it be assumed—until he meets treasure in the shape of something rare, something hitherto untreasured, or something which he can persuade a living author to autograph. From that point, given luck and persistence, he never looks back without complacency.

The point about secondhand bookselling is that the bookseller has not to maintain a stock of new books, has not to interview publishers' travellers or the wayward non-purchaser. He is an individual, his own master, dealing more and more self-reliantly, the farther he advances, in the imperishable. What seller of new books ever hesitates to part with any item in his stock? Is he not thankful to see its back? Is not his one qualm a doubt of the wisdom of any re-order? But the secondhand bookseller can refuse to sell, because he likes to have that particular book on his shelves, in his hands, in his home. He values it; perhaps he regards it as a talisman. "I shan't let it go!" says he.

What a contrast! The secondhand dealer may grow learned in imprints and states, or he may specialise, or he may accumulate and disperse whole libraries; but his customers, once the first of them are satisfied and he has begun to build a stock, are as different as possible from the waverers who sidle into new bookshops wondering if this or that, or a calendar, or perhaps a shawl or a pair of mittens, would give Auntie Jane the more appreciative aged pleasure. His customers are men—often less learned than himself—who know what they want. Some of them may outreach him; some may prize the merest misprints and misplaced lines, the accidents which feed a collector's pride in singularity; but whatever literary rubble and rubbish is included in the secondhand bookseller's purchases can somehow be sold, and if he is worth his salt the man himself is a true collector. He loves what he deals in.

And he has to deal with some queer fish. I remember one old man—he worked at Chatto and Windus—who arrived at the office every morning carrying a dozen or more volumes which he had acquired as he walked down Charing Cross Road from his bus-stop at the Horseshoe in Tottenham Court Road. He hissed his way proudly along the long, rack-lined corridor at 111 St Martin's Lane. He dumped the books on his desk, flung off his overcoat, passed his hands several times through his lint-white locks, to give them the proper tousling, and became as engrossed in his treasure as the miser in *Les Cloches de Cornville*.

Very well; that is what happens if the booklover walks down Charing Cross Road. This one, whose name was Hytch, and who had been a reader for the printing firm of Spottiswoodes before he joined Andrew Chatto, used often to stay for a chat with old Bertram Dobell, the discoverer (I almost said, the inventor) of Thomas Traherne; but his hands did not disdain the dishevelled masses in twopenny and sixpenny boxes of discards, and he was proudest of all if he found something there that he wanted. What he specially wanted, I never found out: I suspect he destroyed many books for the sake of extra-illustrating others. He boasted that there was no room to sit down in his home; that all the chairs and tables were piled with books; and as he also boasted that he let everything, weeds and all, grow in his garden, I always pictured him as suffocated by dust and tottering books in the midst of a wilderness. He is dead; the books he so joyfully acquired are back again in the boxes of discards.

This is another point about the secondhand book trade: that its material is constantly returning to circulation, none the worse for being older than it was at the previous venture. New books may languish on the publishers' shelves; the lucky ones sell out; anything which has been published for a week becomes an excellent bargain for the secondhand trade. I knew one volume of greatly praised poems which as a "first edition, mint" fetched half a guinea, when copies of that same first edition lay quite still at the publisher's and might have been bought there for six shillings. Only publisher and author suffered; and both, fortunately, were men of humour.

As a contrast, let me recall the strange case of the secondhand bookseller who allowed himself to become a literary critic. This was in 1923, when Aldous Huxley had just made the earliest of his reputations. The bookseller apparently disliked Huxley's work very much. Instead of rejoicing in the possession of a first edition, and offering it at double the published price (as other dealers were legitimately doing), he rudely diminished its value. HUXLEY, ALDOUS, said he, LIMBO. FIRST EDITION. Published 5s. net. MY PRICE, 4d. I need hardly say that those who rushed to secure the bargain had no success.

I remember seeing the princes of the trade grouped at a sale at which, as a boy of sixteen, I had been told to bid. It was my notion of a witenagemot; myself far from wisdom. Therefore the lot passed over my head. It included an edition of *The Pilgrim's Progress* with Flaxman illustrations which J. M. Dent wanted, and I was on no account to spend more than a pound. The lot fetched twenty-five shillings; so I was defeated and in danger of being disgraced. However, the purchaser—Dobell—with much good nature let me have the Flaxman for three-and-sixpence. I came out a conqueror.

Since 1901 other dealers in secondhand masterpieces have filled the shopping space in Charing Cross Road. They overflow into the courts leading east to St Martin's Lane, and, as one goes north, down the streets on both sides of the road also. Towards the Oxford Street end stands one of the really extraordinary enterprises of the book world—Foyles. Two brothers began this shop within the memory of many who are living now. By some genius they have made it the busiest centre for the sale of books known to me. One may go at any time of day into any of the departments—and there seems no end to them—and find everywhere a packed concentration of students seeking books and advice. The atmosphere is that of great, preoccupied busyness; the assistants are inexhaustible encyclopaedias; whole ranges of cheap classics, new school books, histories, dictionaries, novels, and in fact everything, as far as everything can now be obtained, is at hand for the student's need. There is, of course, a rare book department in Foyles, where those more exclusive in taste can rove; but for the most part this is a store for men and women of small means in search of essential tools. As an institution it is overwhelming.

4 *Remainders; various booksellers; the problem of space*

It may be complained that my view of the book trade as shown here is partial. I confess it. I have personally no taste for the luxurious, and much as I admire handsomely printed tomes in splendid bindings—by the way, if you step a little way up Shaftesbury Avenue as it goes towards Bloomsbury from Cambridge Circus you will see the premises of one of the great London firms of fine binders, Zaehnsdorf—I do not wish to possess them. I have been a publisher; I am now a professional writer; therefore I care most for what is printed in books and am more interested in what scholars have done than in what aid the printers and binders have lent to their work. The work of scholars may call for care rather than genius; but this care is very excellent and of a value to booklovers which cannot be exaggerated.

John Sewell

James Asperne

Both of Cornhill

Robert Dodsley

J. Lackington, "the Cobbler
turned Bookseller"

Georgian Booksellers

All the Books at Foyle's

Rare Books at Hatchards: the late A. L. Humphreys

Alas! The rewards of scholars are small, and the disappointments innumerable. I have spent hours in Holborn, relishing in the window of Glaishers' bookshop—destroyed during the war—copies of books "remaindered" or sold off cheap by their publishers; and I do not consider those hours to have been wasted. They have taught me, among other lessons, that the work of the scholar may be, to publishers, a cause of greater gloom than the work of the novelist. For the remainder is not quite secondhand. It is a book of which some man—some partnership of men—has lost hope.

One or two booksellers about the country have specialised in remainders; Glaishers would seem to be the most central among them. Otherwise, whether new or secondhand, books are to be found everywhere in central London between Hammersmith and Bishopsgate, between Knightsbridge and the Tower. There is a fine shop for the sale of new books near Victoria Station; there was once, until it was demolished to make room for buildings on the South Bank, a favourite shop of mine—hardly more than a cupboard in size— close to Waterloo where I picked up necessities in secondhand books. Several shops are gone from Waterloo Bridge; Great Turnstile, near Lincoln's Inn, has lost its former glory, but you may find Hollings in Great Queen Street, across Kingsway. Do not forget, also, to look on the south side of New Oxford Street, between Tottenham Court Road and the West Central Post Office, for what you may at first suppose to be a small shop devoted to the store and sale of the novels of Dickens in their original parts. The name is Spencer. Behind that unostentatious frontage lies the most remarkable collection of prints, especially coloured prints, in this or any other city. The original Spencer has been long dead; but his successors carry on a grand tradition, and the stock here is magnificent. Museum Street and Bury Street, leading directly to the British Museum, have their shops, especially for foreign classics; and Great Russell Street, where leading publishers command the stars, is a home also for bookshops of even higher aspirations. So Charing Cross Road has not a complete monopoly, even of the secondhand trade. It is only a centre; a centre not inferior in its concentration to anything else in the world.

But what all these London bookshops are short of is space. One reason why Foyles attract such crowds of students is that they offer a whole building full of books, whereas many of the other dealers have nothing to show explorers but a small front shop in which one cannot turn or stand back from shelves to see what is ranged above.

It is otherwise in American cities, where there is unlimited space; in London one must be a booklover indeed to work and seek treasures in kennels. How fortunate for us that the trade is full of men who, however bitterly they may write and speak of publishers and self-advertising authors, do in fact read books, praise them, and in the quietness of their homes love them.

V

Literary Homes

1 *Milton and Hazlitt; Blake; the migrations of Authors; and their Geography*

Do not be alarmed. This chapter, far from suggesting a method of general superannuation, only shows how the same streets in London, even the same houses—or houses built on the sites of other houses—have accommodated the authors of many generations. William Hazlitt rented from 1812 to 1819 a house in Westminster which was known as No. 19 York Street. The house belonged to Jeremy Bentham; and the man who lived in it before Hazlitt was James Mill. Long before, between 1652 and 1660, when York Street was called Petty France, No. 19 was occupied by John Milton. Hazlitt placed on the parapet of the house a stone tablet, bearing the words "Sacred to Milton, Prince of Poets"; but alas the tablet could not preserve the house. Those who came after esteemed neither great poets nor great essayists. They demolished the sacred dwelling and built in its place the block of flats we know as Queen Anne's Mansions.

Milton, like other London authors, moved from house to house and from district to district. He was born in Bread Street, Cheapside; and once he had returned from Italy I doubt if he was ever long away from London. He settled first in St Bride's Churchyard and afterwards in Lamb Alley, Aldersgate, which may have been the home of his married sister. I do not know where he lived after his marriage, unless it was in that house in Holborn the back of which communicated with Lincoln's Inn Fields; but in days of political greatness, when he was appointed in 1649 Latin Secretary to the Council of State, he had an official residence in Scotland Yard. Three years later he moved to Petty France.

He was still there at the Restoration, when he took refuge with a friend in Bartholomew Close; but he quite soon had a home of his own again, and in 1666, shortly before the outbreak of the Great Fire, he was in Artillery Walk, Bunhill Fields. It was from this address that the manuscript of *Paradise Lost* was submitted to the Archbishop of Canterbury; it was to this address that Thomas Tomkyns, the

Archbishop's chaplain and official censor, sent reluctant permission for the poem to be printed. Milton, as far as I know, remained in Artillery Walk until he died eight years later.

His moves resemble those of nearly all authors who have lived in London. Few such have stayed long in one place. Carlyle, who in spite of his conjugal problems was forty-six years in Cheyne Row, did so; but Carlyle had chosen wisely. The house was a hundred and fifty years old when he took it, and was thought likely to outlast "three races of these modern fashionables." It still stands. William Blake lodged for seventeen years in South Molton Street, and left only because his landlord went abroad. Macaulay was fifteen years in the Albany; Monckton Milnes fourteen at 26 Pall Mall; Samuel Butler thirty-eight in Clifford's Inn; and Swinburne thirty at The Pines, Putney. But these are exceptions; and even the constant Blake had at least five London homes besides his birthplace, which was No. 28 Broad Street, Carnaby Market, near Great Marlborough Street. He was in Green Street, Leicester Square; Poland Street, running south from Oxford Street; had a whole fine eight-or-ten-roomed house, which he kept until it was burgled, in Hercules Buildings, Lambeth (Hogarth also once lived in Lambeth); was in lodgings again in South Molton Street; and—this was the last—in chambers at No. 3 Fountain Court, Strand.

All are interesting addresses. And since Blake was the first writer of genius to settle beside the South Bank of the Thames (when Cowley went to Battersea to get away from the Court it was a country village), I want to remark a curious fact. It is that while in Elizabethan and Jacobean days the dramatists and poets naturally lived in or just outside the City, within reach of St Paul's, the next generations of writers followed the town, and more particularly the *ton*, west. You find them close to St James's rather than St Paul's, with the Inns of Court and the Strand as an eastern boundary to high culture. Books and pamphlets might be printed in the City; and Grub Street, in Moorfields, was where all hack pamphleteers were supposed to live. But when Congreve disgusted Voltaire by priding himself on breeding rather than genius his pride meant that no Augustan wit dreamed of earning bread directly by his pen. Even Dryden—"not a very genteel man," according to Pope—had his eyes on the Court, and stayed no longer than necessary near Fleet Street. Of his immediate successors only Defoe lived east of Temple Bar.

However, certain changes occurred in the social structure after

Queen Anne's death. Sir Robert Walpole did not employ wits to write his pamphlets; he pretended to be a bluff Norfolk squire, and he tightened the political censorship of plays and books. The patron, except in rare instances, had gone. Places and pensions were more sparsely bestowed upon authors. So a later generation than Swift's and Congreve's, while continuing to frequent Soho or Covent Garden or Leicester Square, spread back again towards St Paul's, where lay the publishers on whom their livelihood depended.

London had then only lately begun to expand to the north. Plans drawn in the reign of Queen Anne show, east of the City, Stepney as a country village; west, as soon as High Holborn is passed, the dwellings end; north of Holborn there is a fringe of streets among which an outline of Clerkenwell Road is just to be caught; and north of Piccadilly almost nothing urban lies beyond Golden Square. Sixty years later, according to Fanny Burney, when, as Blake was to do in 1789, her family lived in Poland Street,

"Oxford Road, as at that time Oxford Street was called . . . had little on its further side but fields, gardeners' grounds, or unculti-vated suburbs. Portman, Manchester, Russell, Belgrave Squares, Portland Place, etc., had not yet a single stone or brick laid."

It is true that one may over-emphasise the movement east because of Dr Johnson's association with Fleet Street (I shall come to that, and to the Doctor's nomadism, presently), and Boswell as a young man freely ranged the West End. But Boswell was not a professional author; he was a youth of family. If his passion for the best talk had been smaller he would have stayed permanently in Whitehall and Mayfair. Goldsmith, like Johnson, was a writer by trade; though he moved often he never moved west. His true London home was an early one, Green Arbour Court, Old Bailey, from which a man went down into Seacoal Lane by way of Breakneck Steps.

It was William Hazlitt, among the professionals, who first showed impatient waywardness in his addresses. They seem indifferently to have taken him east, west, and back again, as if he could settle nowhere. At his first coming to London he was at 139 Long Acre, with his elder brother. From 1799 until 1803 he was at No. 12 Rathbone Place; and from 1804 to 1807 in Great Russell Street. He then moved to No. 34 Southampton Buildings; to Westminster, where he celebrated Milton and stayed for seven years; and back in 1820 to No. 9 South-ampton Buildings, where he first saw the faithless Sally Walker. He

77

was in Down Street, Piccadilly, from 1824 until 1827; at 40 Half Moon Street, Piccadilly, in 1828 (it is startling to think that Henry James, only fifty years after, was at No. 7); in Bouverie Street, which runs down from Fleet Street to the Thames, in 1829; and finally at No. 6 Frith Street, Soho, where he died in 1830.

By Hazlitt's time, St Paul's had become a place of pilgrimage rather than a centre of employment for needy scribblers. Bloomsbury was in being; Pentonville, Islington, Euston, Camden Town, Edmonton, Highgate, and Hampstead all gave shelter to bookmen, and the bookmen had many more miles of roads and houses at their disposal. They sometimes moved because they wished to be nearer friends; sometimes because they could not well pay their rent. Sometimes, living in frowsy furnished lodgings, they moved because they had developed a horror of their apartments.

2 Moorfields and St Paul's Churchyard

Since Goering's fire raid on London, the district around St Paul's Cathedral, at first a mass of rubble, has been gradually opened to the eye. And in strolling near Moorgate I have often thought of a picture drawn by the earliest of all historians of London, William Fitzstephen, who wrote in the twelfth century. It is like a painting by Bruegel.

"When the great fen, or moor, which watereth the walls of the city on the north side, is frozen, many young men play upon the ice; some, striding as wide as they may, do slide swiftly; others make themselves seats of ice, as great as millstones; one sits down, many hand in hand to draw him, and, one slipping on a sudden, all fall together; some tie bones to their feet and under their heels; and, shoving themselves by a little picked staff, do slide as swiftly as a bird flieth in the air, or an arrow out of a cross-bow."

From that to references in Ben Jonson, Pepys, Ned Ward, and Defoe is a rapid journey. I see the open ground, the wrestling, the marchings and combats, the conjurors and bookstalls, and the great revivalist meetings of Wesley and Whitefield which caused Moorfields—before they were lost under buildings—to be famous among all Londoners; and something at least of the London which our ancestors knew. It must have been like this after the first Great Fire of London, when Pepys, meeting his bookseller, learned that

78

"the goods laid in St Paul's Churchyarde fired through the windows those in St Faith's Church; and those coming to the warehouses' doors fired them, and burned all the books and the pillars of the church.... He do believe there is above £150,000 of books burned; all the great booksellers almost undone: not only these, but their warehouses at their Hall, and under Christchurch, and elsewhere being all burned. A great want thereof there will be of books, specially Latin books and foreign books; and, among others, the Polyglottes and new Bible, which he believes will be presently worth £40 a-piece."

As in 1666, so in our own time! And in these days as in those the ground laid bare. Pepys went to see it, as we went to see it, while the wreckage still burned. But it was a friend of mine who made the comment that Pepys might have made. He said disconsolately: "The rubble of famous buildings is horribly like any other rubble."

As we know, the city was built up again; Moorfields, where fugitives from the Fire had camped on the grass, were covered; publishers came again to the neighbourhood of St Paul's (which was itself rebuilt), and were greater than ever. Before the century had closed, Ned Ward observed that in St Paul's Churchyard

"booksellers were as plenty as pedlars at a fair, and parsons in their shops were busily searching after the venerable conceits of our worm-eaten ancestors, as if they came thither for want of brains."

And Gay, in 1716, wrote that

> Volumes on shelter'd Stalls expanded lye,
> And various Science lures the learned Eye;
> The bending Shelves with pond'rous Scholiasts groan,
> And deep Divines to modern Shops unknown:
> Here, like the Bee, that on industrious Wing,
> Collects the various Odours of the Spring,
> Walkers, at leisure, Learning's Flow'rs may spoil,
> Nor watch the Wasting of the Midnight Oil,
> May Morals snatch from Plutarch's tatter'd Page,
> A mildewed Bacon, or Stagyra's Sage.

3 Ned Ward's and Gay's London; Swift

The London of the first years of the eighteenth century must have resembled the backgrounds of engravings by Hogarth and his lesser rivals. It was recognisably a town of contrasted social levels. There were the gentry, laced, frocked, and wigged, carrying swords or canes;

there were the sober shopkeepers and merchants; there was the boisterous stinking rabble. We are well bustled among filth and crowds by Ned Ward, who kept the King's Head Tavern in Fulwood's Rents, near Gray's Inn, and had a taverner's relish for unmitigated sensation. But when we come to Steele or Gay we reach elegance.

Gay's London, indeed, was less a town of rumpus than one of sedan chairs; a town in which, he says, a cane in the hand helps one to keep the wall, and, by its warning to the drivers of passing coaches, forbids them to spatter one from head to foot with mud. Outside White's Club in St James's Street, "the harnessed chair-man idly stands," while others

> In gilded Chariots loll at Ease,
> And lazily insure a Life's Disease;
> While softer Chairs the tawdry Load convey
> To Court, to White's, Assemblies, or the Play.

And since he was personally full of good humour, and had a liking for luxury and great friends, it is of splendours past and present that he is most commendatory. "Come," he says,

> Come, let us leave the the Temple's silent Walls,
> Me business to my distant Lodging calls:
> Through the long Strand together let us stray,
> With Thee conversing, I forget the Way.
> Behold that narrow Street, which steep descends,
> Whose Building to the slimy Shore extends;
> Here Arundel's fam'd Structure rear'd its Frame,
> The Street alone retains an empty Name:
> Where Titian's glowing Paint the Canvas warm'd,
> And Raphael's fair Design, with Judgment, charm'd,
> Now hangs the Bell-man's Song, and pasted here,
> The colour'd Prints of Overton appear.
> Where Statues breath'd, the work of Phidias' Hands,
> A wooden Pump, or lonely Watch-house stands,
> There Essex' stately Pile adorn'd the Shore,
> There Cecil's, Bedford's, Viller's [sic], now no more.
> Yet Burlington's fair Palace still remains;
> Beauty within, without Proportion reigns.
> Beneath his Eye declining Art revives,
> The Wall with animated Picture lives;
> There Handel strikes the Strings, the melting Strain
> Transports the Soul, and thrills through ev'ry Vein;
> There oft I enter (but with cleaner Shoes)
> For Burlington's belov'd by ev'ry Muse.

Burlington, it should be said, was the house of the Duchess of Queensberry, in Burlington Gardens, where Gay (it is almost his only recorded London address) spent a great deal of time, and where he died. In extolling it he claimed familiarity with very aristocratic quarters indeed.

He loved aristocratic quarters. He was a natural inhabitant of other and richer people's homes. He was offered hospitality; and he took it. According to Congreve, he so much loved eating that his motto should have been *edit, ergo est*. And, like others in an age when authors could not afford to be independent, he coveted official posts. One or two of these were found for him; when a third was offered, as Gentleman Usher to a little princess, he refused it as beneath his dignity. But he belonged to the group we know as The Wits; and, if none of these venerated his talents, he was so easy and so good humoured that they helped him with his work and delighted in his triumphs.

The London, described in *Trivia*, which ran to applaud *The Beggar's Opera*, was the London known to Dryden, who had just died at his house in Gerrard Street, "the fifth door on the left hand coming from Newport Street." It was the London which saw the fall of Marlborough after unsurpassed service to his country. It was the London of Robert Harley, Earl of Oxford, and Henry St John, Viscount Bolingbroke; two colleagues who, having successfully intrigued against Marlborough, were soon sundered by their own rivalry and differing temperaments. It was the London of Congreve, Addison, Steele, and Colley Cibber; of Swift, Arbuthnot, Rowe, Prior, and Atterbury; of Warburton and Pope. It was the London of that much less fashionable gentleman, who was little seen in the West End, Daniel Defoe.

Swift was in it because he had been sent by the Irish bishops to try to get for their church certain sums appropriated by the British Crown under the name of First-Fruits and Twentieths. Having failed on an earlier visit, he came again in 1710 with two ambitions. The immediate one was success in his ostensible errand; the second was to secure for himself what he knew to be intellectually his right, a bishopric or at least an English deanery.

He lodged first in Pall Mall; but

"to-morrow I change my lodgings in Pall Mall for one in Bury Street, where I suppose I shall continue while I stay in London "

At Bury Street

"I have the first floor, a dining-room, and bedchamber, at eight shillings a week; plaguy deep, but I spend nothing for eating, never go to a tavern, and very seldom in a coach; yet after all it will be expensive."

Addison was then his best friend in town, owing to a previous acquaintance in Ireland; so he often visited Addison's country home at Chelsea, went with him to coffee-houses, and walked with him in St James's Park and Pall Mall. You can picture them together, with a third member of the group, Addison in some elegance, tall, fine-wigged, and indulgent, turning affectionately to the friend who, he said, had "an inexhaustible Fund of Discourse"; Swift, no less affectionate, because even when they had been cooled by events, "I yet know of no man half so agreeable to me as Addison," but shorter—"a plump man, just five feet five inches high; not very neatly dressed, in a black gown with pudding-sleeves,"—and Nicholas Rowe, the dramatist, "a very pretty sort of man," "of a comely personage," who "would laugh all day long—he would do nothing but laugh." All three laughed.

Addison, Congreve, and Rowe were Whigs. So was Richard Steele a Whig. Swift also, at his arrival, was a Whig; and at heart he was a Whig to the end of his days. He realised, however, that in the matter of First-Fruits and the bishopric Whigs would do nothing for him. Godolphin was "altogether short, dry, and morose." He did not know that Godolphin had already been told to break his staff of office as Lord High Treasurer. "I am almost vowing revenge."

Having been introduced to Harley by Erasmus Lewis, Swift formed what he believed to be a close friendship with the new Chancellor of the Exchequer (afterwards Lord High Treasurer in Godolphin's place); and he observed with glee that

"'tis good to see what a lamentable confession the Whigs make me of my ill-usage; but I mind them not. I am already represented to Harley as a discontented person that was used ill for not being Whig enough; and I hope for good usage from him. The Tories drily tell me, I may make my fortune, if I please; but I do not understand them—or rather, I do understand them."

He understood them. He understood that as power came from the Crown and the small class composed either of the hereditary nobility or the ambitious politicians it was necessary to stand well with that

82

class. He improved his acquaintance with Harley and St John, liked and admired both of them (liked, especially, the procrastinating, gravel-tortured Harley; admired as a prodigy the dazzling thirty-one-year-old St John); and was flattered and used by both.

His rooms in Bury Street proved to have "a thousand stinks," so he moved again to a street which was swept away in 1815, when Waterloo Place was planned.

"I came home to my new lodgings in St Alban's Street, where I pay the same rent, eight shillings a week, for an apartment two pair of stairs; but I have the use of the parlour to receive persons of quality."

"Persons of quality": he was in the swim. He dined constantly with Harley, "My Lord Treasurer," in Dover Street, and less often with St John, lodging in the same street. The three put their heads together over that most imposing of all partisan documents, *The Conduct of the Allies*; in reward Swift gained for the Irish bishops all that he had been sent to get. A patriot and a loyal churchman, he was then a party man; and as much by his ruthlessness on behalf of Harley and St John as by his early *Tale of a Tub* he spoiled his clerical reputation.

He was as proud as Lucifer himself, rejected money that was slipped to him by My Lord Treasurer, sent a hot reply to a lord who complained of something which he had not written for *The Examiner*, and refused to have any more to do with this lord until his pardon had been begged. He grudged every one of the half-crowns which in those days visitors had to give to "lying footmen" who said their masters were not within; but he would not omit one of them. His deafness grew and his dizziness became frequent and alarming. He was attacked by a violent form of shingles. But in pursuit of his objects he stayed in London, moving from Bury Street to Chelsea and from Chelsea to Suffolk Street, Pall Mall, and again from Suffolk Street ("not liking a ground floor, nor the ill smell and other circumstances") to St Martin's Street. Leicester Square, where he had to pay ten shillings a week; and later to what is called a health resort at Kensington Gravel Pits, and back to a single room in Ryder Street, St James's. He would not leave until the Peace was signed and his own fate decided. In the end, as is known, after endless delays and humiliations, he received the Deanery of St Patrick's, which meant exile and the fact that the great men were done with him.

Swift, said Pope, had "an odd, blunt way, that is mistaken, by strangers, for ill-nature." And he went on to illustrate the oddness and bluntness—which rose from ferocious pride—by a story recognisable by us as a parable. Here it is:

"There's no describing it but by facts," said Pope. "I'll tell you one that just comes into my head. One evening Gay and I went to see him: you know how intimately we were all acquainted. On our coming in; 'Hey-day, gentlemen,' says the Doctor, 'What's the meaning of this visit? How come you to leave all the great lords that you are so fond of, to come hither to see a poor Dean?'—Because we would rather see you than any of them.—'Aye, any one, that did not know you so well as I do, might believe you. But, since you are come, I must get some supper for you, I suppose?'—No, Doctor, we have supped already.—'Supped already! That's impossible: why, 'tis not eight o'clock yet.'—Indeed we have—'That's very strange: but if you had not supped, I must have got something for you.—Let me see, what should I have had? a couple of lobsters? Ay, that would have done very well;—two shillings: tarts; a shilling. But you will drink a glass of wine with me, though you supped so much before your usual time, only to spare my pocket?'—no, we had rather talk with you, than drink with you.—'But if you had supped with me, as in all reason you ought to have done, you must have drank with me.—A bottle of wine; two shillings.—Two and two, is four; and one is five: just two and six-pence a piece. There, Pope, there's half-a-crown for you; and there's another for you, sir: for I won't save anything by you I am determined.' This was all said and done with his usual seriousness on such occasions; and in spite of every thing we could say to the contrary, he actually obliged us to take the money."

4 The Wits; Steele; no more Court Patronage; the Booksellers

Swift's true companions were the wits. Besides Congreve, prematurely old, blind, and gouty, Addison, Steele, the laughing Rowe, and Ambrose ("Pastoral" or "Namby Pamby") Philips, he loved best and was most entirely at ease with Matthew Prior, Dr Garth (author of a satire called The Dispensary, who delivered Dryden's funeral oration), Arbuthnot, Atterbury, and Pope. These men, over a long period, met often to make fun of the rest of the world; and Arbuthnot's work was sometimes indistinguishable in destructive ridicule from Swift's own. Swift called it "very pretty."

Atterbury, the most reverend of this company, lived in Church

"Work", by Ford Madox Brown. Heath Street, Hampstead, with portraits of Carlyle and Maurice on the right. Reproduced by kind permission of Manchester City Art Gallery

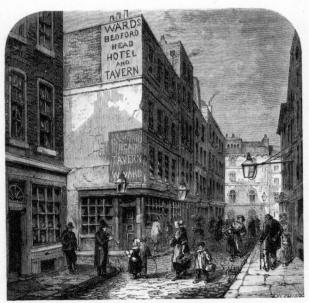

The old "Bedford Head" in Southampton Street, Strand

Charles Lamb's Colebrooke Row, Islington

Horace Walpole's Library, Strawberry Hill

Lane, Chelsea; and in April, 1711, Swift, who needed better air and more exercise than his life in the West End allowed, decided to move to Chelsea. It was his intention to walk backwards and forwards to and from London, which he did, the journey taking him, on one occasion, "something less than an hour." He pretended that it needed five thousand, seven hundred, and forty-eight steps; and in hot weather it "made your fat little Presto sweat in the forehead." His lodging, half a mile farther from the town than it should have been, was "over against Dr Atterbury's house." At the first coming,

"I got here," he says, "in the stage coach with Patrick (his servant) and my portmanteau for sixpence, and pay six shillings a week for one silly room with confounded coarse sheets."

The sheets mattered a great deal; because it was Swift's habit to write to Stella from bed, sometimes at night, sometimes in the early morning. He was generally in bed by eleven, wearing a velvet night-cap; and he told Stella that he was up and at work in his dressing-gown, between six and seven o'clock in the morning. Dean Lockier, however, another of the wits, and the man who, as a youth, dared to correct Dry-den at Will's Coffee-house, said Swift lay abed till eleven o'clock, think-ing of wit for the day. Both accounts may be true—of different days. All that matters is that when he was to be with the wits Swift was happy.

They met, for the most part, at each other's homes, at Pope's, Atterbury's, and Arbuthnot's rather than elsewhere. Congreve was not far away, at his address in Surrey Street, Strand; Peterborough, the wild general who was also a wit and a man of talent, and although "the ramblingest lying rogue on earth," "loved difficulties and was famous for doing great things with small means," was in Bolton Street, Piccadilly; and Arbuthnot, for seven years from 1714 until 1721, was in Dover Street, a stone's-throw away. Pope, who had been at school in London, and had been reintroduced to the town by the age-ing Wycherley, had at that time no London address. He lived with his father at Binfield, near Wokingham. It was not until 1716 that his father moved to Chiswick, and not until two years later that Pope had a home of his own, the famous villa at Twickenham. He stayed in Dover Street or St James's Street or in a now-destroyed thoroughfare called Cleveland Court, St James's.

Arbuthnot, the creator of an imaginary character named Martinus Scriblerus, to whose "Club" the wits belonged, and to whose *Memoirs* they all, including Harley himself, contributed, wrote to Pope in 1714:

"Martin's office is now the second door on the left hand in Dover Street, where he will be glad to see Dr Parnell, Mr Pope, and his old friends, to whom he can still afford half a pint of claret."

Spence says:

"The design of the Memoirs of Scriblerus was to have ridiculed all the false tastes in learning, under the character of a man of capacity enough; that had dipped into every art and science, but injudiciously in each. . . . It was from a part of these memoirs that Mr Swift took his first hints for Gulliver."

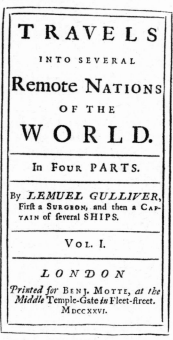

TRAVELS

INTO SEVERAL

Remote NATIONS

OF THE

WORLD.

In FOUR PARTS.

By *LEMUEL GULLIVER*,
First a SURGEON, and then a CAP-
TAIN of several SHIPS.

VOL. I.

LONDON

Printed for BENJ. MOTTE, *at the*
Middle Temple-Gate *in* Fleet-street.
MDCCXXVI.

Titlepage of the First Edition of
Swift's *Gulliver's Travels* (1726)

Richard Steele was not a contributor to the *Memoirs*. This talented, sanguine, and improvident Irishman had been by turns soldier, Christian, gentleman-waiter to the Queen's husband, reformer of the stage, and (with Addison's collaboration) writer of the most famous periodical essays of all time, which were published in various series under the titles of *The Tatler, The Spectator, The Guardian*, and *The English-*

man. When these essays dealt with manners, they were written with an incomparably merry eye and easy pen; when they ventured, as the later ones increasingly did, into politics, they were ferociously partisan. That was a mistake. Swift, having quarrelled with him, said Steele was the worst company in the world until he had a bottle of wine in his head; and complained that he was abominably governed by his wife.

When we first hear of Steele in London, he is living in Smith Street, Westminster; but when Addison had country quarters in Chelsea, Steele also stayed there, "by the water-side." He then lodged in Bury Street, "at the third house, right hand, turning out of Jermy Street" (these cumbrous directions to postmen and visitors were necessary until street numbering became general about 1674); and it was the landlady of this house who is supposed to have had him arrested for unpaid rent.

In 1712 Steele took a house in Bloomsbury Square, about which he wrote to his wife "you cannot conceive how pleased I am that I shall have the prettiest house to receive the prettiest woman who is the darling of Richard Steele." He was very happy there. Unfortunately he spent everything he earned, and his earnings were irregular; so that he was not always free to enjoy his wife's company.

"Dear Prue," he wrote to her. "I enclose five guineas, but can't come home to dinner. Dear little woman, take care of thyself, and eat and drink cheerfully."

"My dear" (on another occasion), "I shall not come home to dinner, but have fixed everything; and received money for present uses. I desire, my dear, that you have nothing else to do but be a darling; the way to which is to be always in good humour, and believe I spend none of my time but to the advantage of you."

While in this house in Bloomsbury Square, according to Thackeray, whose authority is not given, he turned inconvenient bailiffs into footmen to wait upon his guests; and after the death of his "Dear Prue," who before marriage had been "Dear, lovely Mrs Scurlock," he was in Villiers Street, Strand. This was his last address in London.

Long before then, however, the calamity which Swift had laboured to avert had arrived; and Harley and St John had split asunder. Worse still, from Swift's point of view, Queen Anne had died, St John had lost his nerve, Whig peers had acted with extraordinary resolution, and the political scene was transformed. Harley went to the Tower;

Robert Walpole became head of affairs; Marlborough had one peep of revived glory, in the course of which he obtained for Steele (Cibber says at the request of the managers, to whom Steele behaved with great generosity) the post of director of the Theatre Royal. There were no more bailiffs, no more arrests for debt. And once again English letters suffered a change. The wits gave place to the realists, who looked no longer towards Dover Street and My Lord Treasurer, but towards Fleet Street and St Paul's Churchyard, where Cave, Davies, and the Newberys held sway as legitimate rivals or successors to Tonson, Curll, Lintot, and the original Dodsley.

5 Horace Walpole; Gray; Strawberry Hill

Five writers do not support what I have just said. Young, a pensionary of Walpole's and all his life asking for more money, was a country rector whose Night Thoughts had no connection with politics; Shenstone, "the water-gruel bard," was a small northern landowner who sometimes stayed at "Mr Winkle's, perfumer, at the King's Arms by Temple Bar, Fleet Street"; and Akenside was a physician who, besides practising in Hampstead as well as in town (he lived in Craven Street and Bloomsbury Square), subsisted comfortably on a pension provided by a rich friend. He is portrayed in Peregrine Pickle as having "all the uncouth gravity and supercilious conceit of a physician piping hot from his studies," and is forthwith made very ridiculous indeed. There remained two great men who could afford to be indifferent to literary earnings and the vagaries of political favour. One was a scholar; the other the Prime Minister's son.

Otherwise court favour was no longer a magnet; with the coming of daily newspapers to which arguing letters might be addressed the controversial pamphlet declined in importance; and in the absence of patronage genius was driven to find its own level. Sir Robert Walpole was no friend to writers. He offered Pope a pension, which was refused. He pensioned Young. He sent bank-notes to Richard Savage. And, to please a friend, he sceptically made Congreve a Commissioner of Customs, saying that he doubted if Congreve had any head for business. His own head was all for business. He thoughtfully provided a number of remunerative posts for his son Horace, the work connected with which was done by underlings. Horace drew the salaries; and the world possesses in his letters and set pieces of reminiscence a record of eighteenth century politics, gentility, and personalities which most of

us find so enchanting that we do not grudge him a penny of his un-
earned pensions.

He lived to be almost an octogenarian, having been born in Septem-
ber, 1717, in Arlington Street, St James's, where his father then lived.
He afterwards occupied another house in Arlington Street, and one in
Grosvenor Square. Those I think were his only addresses in town.
And all his life he remembered the fact that "I was born at the top of
the world." This birth enabled him to be the perfect dilettante.

"Pray, my dear child" (he writes to his kinsman, Sir Horace Mann),
"don't compliment me any more upon my learning; there is nobody
so superficial. Except a little history, a little poetry, a little painting,
and some divinity, I know nothing. How should I? I, who have
always lived in the big, busy world; who lie a-bed all the morning
calling it morning as long as you please; who sup in company;
who have played at pharaoh half my life, and now at loo till two
or three in the morning; who have always loved pleasure; haunted
auctions—in short, who don't know as much astronomy as would
carry me to Knightsbridge, nor more physic than a physician, nor
in short anything that is called science. If it were not that I lay up a
little provision in summer, like the ant, I should be as ignorant as
all the people I live with."

It also enabled him to pretend—it was no more than pretence—
to be ignorant of all that went on at the other end of the town:

"I have no thirst to know the rest of my contemporaries, from the
absurd bombast of Dr Johnson down to the silly Dr Goldsmith;
though the latter changeling has had bright gleams of parts, and the
former had sense, till he changed it for words, and sold it for a pension. Don't think me scornful. Recollect that I have seen Pope, and
lived with Gray."

He had lived with Gray; that is, he had been with him at Eton,
travelled with him on the Continent, and on that excursion quarrelled
with him to the point of estrangement. Luckily they were reconciled
and were good friends afterwards. From one reference of Gray's,
the occasion of the quarrel may be gathered: "Walpole was son of
the first minister, and you may easily conceive that, on this account,
he might assume an air of superiority." No doubt he did assume such
an air. He called himself "passionate, timid, and vainglorious." He
sometimes denied, and sometimes admitted, that he was capricious.

89

He could be spiteful, and a snob. Hardly anybody except Macaulay has ever been able to resist his vivacity.

He was very thin, "very affected, always aiming at wit," ran into a room "like a peewit," and loved cats and children. In the assessment of men and books he was extraordinarily acute. And as he lived in the reigns of three sovereigns, and at an exceptional vantage point of independence, the observations he stored were priceless. They embraced the growth of London.

"I remember" (he said, when he was nearly sixty) "when my father went out of place, and was to return visits, which Ministers are excused from doing, he could not guess where he was, finding himself in so many new streets and squares. This was thirty years ago. They have been building ever since, and one would think had imported two or three capitals. London could put Florence into its fob-pocket; but as they build so slightly, if they did not rebuild, it would be just the reverse of Rome, a vast circumference of city surrounding an area of ruins. As its present progress is chiefly north, and Southwark marches south, the metropolis promises to be as broad as long. Rows of houses shoot out every way like a polypus; and, so great is the rage of building everywhere, that, if I stay here (Twickenham) a fortnight, without going to town, I look about to see if no new house is built since I went last. . . . This little island will be ridiculously proud some ages hence of its former brave days, and swear its capital was once as big again as Paris, or—what is to be the name of the city that will then give laws to Europe?—perhaps New York or Philadelphia."

By the time he wrote what I have just quoted, Walpole had established himself in the tiny house at Twickenham which he bought from the proprietor of a toy shop and which became famous as Strawberry Hill.

"It is a little play-thing-house that I got out of Mrs Chevenix's shop, and is the prettiest bauble you ever saw. It is set in enamelled meadows, with filligree hedges;

A small Euphrates through the piece is roll'd
And little finches wave their wings in gold.

Two delightful roads, that you would call dusty, supply me continually with coaches and chaises; . . . and Pope's ghost is just now skimming under my window by a most poetical moonlight. . . .

The Chevenixes had tricked it out for themselves: up two pair of stairs is what they call Mr Chevenix's library, furnished with three maps, one shelf, a bust of Sir Isaac Newton, and a lame telescope without any glasses. Lord John Sackville *predecessed* me here, and instituted certain games called *cricketalia*, which have been celebrated this very evening in honour of him in a neighbouring meadow."

The house was his toy. But, besides being the perfect dilettante, Walpole was a great collector of trifles, or what he called "serendipity," the odds and ends of whimsical choice from all arts; and he also illustrated in his practice a strange feature of eighteenth-century fashion. Houses were being built, not only in London, but all over the country; and grounds were being tortured according to extraordinary new plans or extravagant new fads.

"I wish you could see the villas and seats here;" wrote Walpole to his distant friend. "The country wears a new face; everybody is improving their places, and as they don't fortify their plantations with entrenchments of walls and high hedges, one has the benefit of them even in passing by. The dispersed buildings, I mean, temples, bridges, &c., are generally Gothic or Chinese, and give a whimsical air of novelty that is very pleasing. You would like a drawing-room in the latter style that I fancied and have been executing at Mr Rigby's in Essex; it has large and very fine Indian landscapes, with a black fret round them, and round the whole entablature of the room, and all the ground or hanging is of pink paper."

His own taste was for the Gothic; and Strawberry Hill became such a famous museum that the King and Queen and Princesses, all the nobility, all visiting foreigners, and crowds of other curious persons demanded to see it. Those less than royal had to obtain cards of admission—which were often refused. They developed into a nuisance. But the owner's pride in his museum never staled; it stimulated him to the writing of the first Gothic Romance ever to be found in English literature, *The Castle of Otranto*; and it gave him a gratifying social importance which, once he had retired from Parliament, was perhaps a little necessary to his vanity.

If Thomas Gray did not escape the prevailing decorative disease it was because he was a scholar and an antiquary. I do not think he Gothicised his Cambridge quarters; and when he came to London he lived quietly in lodgings, at one period "at Mrs Jauncey's in Southampton Row"; usually in Jermyn Street, over Roberts the hosier's or Frisby the oilman's. What he did was to hunt up treasures for his friends and check their greatest absurdities. "Don't let me," said he, to an over-rabid friend, "when I come gaping into Colman-street, be directed to the Gentleman's at the ten Pinnacles, or with the Church-porch at his door." But he was impressed by Walpole's doings at Strawberry:

"Mr W. has lately made a new bedchamber, which as it is in the best taste of anything he has yet done, and in your own Gothic way, I must describe a little. You enter by a peaked door at one corner of the room (out of a narrow winding passage, you may be sure) into an alcove, in which the bed is to stand, formed by a screen of pierced work opening by one large arch in the middle to the rest of the chamber, which is lighted at the other end by a bow window of three bays, whose tops are of rich painted glass in mosaic. The ceiling is coved and fretted in star and quatrefoil compartments, with roses at the intersections, all in papiermache. The chimney on your left is the high altar in the cathedral of Rouen (from whence the screen also is taken) consisting of a low sur-based arch between two octagon towers, whose pinnacles almost reach the ceiling, all of nich-work. The chairs and dressing-table are real carved ebony, picked up at auctions. The hangings uniform purple paper, hung all over with the court of Henry the Eighth, copied after the Hol-beins in the Queen's closet at Kensington. The bed is to be either from Burleigh (for Lord Exeter is new-furnishing it, and means to sell some of his original household-stuff) of the rich old tarnished embroidery; or, if that is not to be had, and it must be new, it is to be a cut velvet with a dark purple pattern on a stone-colour satin ground, and deep mixed fringes and tassels. There's for you!"

I suppose this to have been the most sumptuous of all authors' homes. Pope's grotto of mirrors was quite out-glittered. However, as you will see, Walpole did no more than lead the fashion in Gothic. There were other fashions, one of which he mentioned in the passage I quoted earlier. This was the Chinese fashion.

6 Goldsmith; Johnson; Hogarth; Reynolds; Fox; Burke; Gibbon; Boswell; Nollekens; Hawkesworth; Hawkins; Thrale; the Burneys; Richardson

It was a particularly ridiculous fashion; and one reason why Walpole disliked Goldsmith may have been that Goldsmith saw and said how ridiculous it was. He made a Chinaman go to visit a fine English lady, "a woman equally distinguished for rank, politeness, taste, and understanding."

"'Bless me!' sparkled the lady. 'Can this be the gentleman that was born so far from home? What an unusual share of *somethingness* in his whole appearance. Lord, how I am charmed with the outlandish cut of his face; how bewitching the exotic breadth of his forehead. . . . Pray, Sir, have you got your chopsticks about you? It will be so pretty to see the meat carried to the mouth with a jerk. Pray speak a little Chinese: I have learned some of the language myself. Lord, have you nothing pretty from China about you; something that one does not know what to do with? I have got twenty things from China that are of no use in the world. Look at those jars, they are of the right pea-green: these are the furniture.' *Dear madam, said I, these, though they may appear fine in your eyes, are but paltry to a Chinese; but, as they are useful utensils, it is proper, they should have a place in every apartment.* 'Useful! Sir,' replied the lady; 'sure you mistake, they are of no use in the world. . . . A Chinese, a traveller, and want taste! It surprises me.'"

Goldsmith came hopefully to London after touring Europe as a young man, with the ambition to practise as a doctor; but he was unlucky. After trying on Bankside to earn a living by medicine he became a druggist's assistant, a printer's reader in the fine Salisbury Square premises of that master printer, Samuel Richardson, and subsequently usher in a school at Peckham. When at last he turned to literature he went to live and work in St Paul's Churchyard as hack reviewer for Ralph Griffiths, the illiterate bookseller who published *The Monthly Review* and used the appropriate sign of "*The Dunciad.*"

This was in 1757, the year of Walpole's anonymous Chinese pamphlet. Three years afterwards it was from John Newbery's shop, also in St Paul's Churchyard, that the first of these *Chinese Letters* which we know as *The Citizen of the World* appeared as a contribution to *The Public Ledger*. It contained Lien Chi Altangi's first impression of London as it appeared to him in 1759; and it refers particularly to the hanging signboards by which, before street numbering, shopkeepers told pedestrians where they were to be found.

"Judge then my disappointment" (says Lien Chi Altangi, pretending that he had expected to find brilliance and gaiety everywhere), "on entering London, to see no signs of that opulence so much talked of abroad; wherever I turn, I am presented with a gloomy solemnity in the houses, the streets and the inhabitants; . . . in the midst of their pavements, a great lazy puddle moves muddily along; heavy laden machines with wheels of unwieldy thickness crowd up every passage; so that a stranger, instead of finding time for observation, is often crushed to pieces.

"The houses borrow very few ornaments from architecture; their chief decoration seems to be a paltry piece of painting, hung out at their doors or windows, at once a proof of their indigence and vanity. Their vanity, in each having one of these pictures exposed to view; and their indigence, in being unable to get them better painted."

Goldsmith had not come from China; but he was a stranger in London. He once in later years startled a group of friends by referring to a time "when I lived among the beggars in Axe Lane"; and his most famous address is the one in Green Arbour Court. Thomas Percy, the collector of *Reliques*, first visited him here; and Washington Irving described the place in a story called *The Club of Queer Fellows*:

"This Green-arbour-court I found to be a small square, of tall and miserable houses, the very intestines of which seemed turned inside out, to judge from the old garments and frippery that fluttered from every window. It appeared to be a region of washerwomen, and lines were stretched about the little square, on which clothes were dangling to dry."

Dr Percy's account takes us within doors:

"The Doctor was writing his *Enquiry*, etc., in a wretched dirty room, in which there was but one chair, and when he, from civility, offered it to his visitant, himself was obliged to sit in the window. While they were conversing, someone gently rapped at the door, and being desired to come in, a poor ragged little girl of very decent behaviour, entered, who, dropping a curtsie, said, 'My mama sends her compliments, and begs the favour of you to lend her a chamber-pot full of coals.'"

Goldsmith's fortunes improved; he removed to Wine Office Court, Fleet Street; and he entertained both Percy and Johnson, whom he had likewise met, to a supper. Johnson astonished Percy by appearing in new clothes and a new wig; and when his garb was remarked he made a very charming and natural reply. "Why, sir," said he; "I hear that Goldsmith, who is a very great sloven, justifies his disregard of cleanliness and decency by quoting my practice; and I am desirous this night to show him a better example."

As Goldsmith was seventeen years younger than Johnson, it was a high compliment. Johnson always set Goldsmith's genius high, though belittling him as a talker. He said Goldsmith was a man who, whatever he wrote, did it better than any other man could do; but when Reynolds suggested that Goldsmith's friends might overrate his work from personal partiality, Johnson replied with truth:

"Nay, Sir, the partiality of his friends was always against him. It was with difficulty we could give him a hearing. Goldsmith had no settled notions upon any subject; so he talked always at random."

Goldsmith thought the impatience of his friends was even surpassed by the indifference of the public. "Whenever I write anything," he complained (in what Boswell calls ludicrous terms of distress), "the public *make a point* to know nothing about it."

He moved to lodgings among the green lanes of Islington, in order to be near Newbery, who lived still farther from town, at Canonbury; and it was here, where Hogarth painted the portrait of his landlady, that he wrote the successful *History of England in a Series of Letters from a Nobleman to his Son*. It was thought to be by Chesterfield—or Lyttelton. Subsequently Goldsmith lodged ignominiously in Garden Court in the Temple, and in Gray's Inn; while in days of plenty, when *The Good Natur'd Man* brought him five hundred unexpected pounds, he bought chambers at No. 2 Brick Court, Middle Temple, and kept them until his death. Visiting long afterwards this most splendid of Goldsmith's homes, Thackeray said that although the rooms contained good carved work the bedroom was a closet without light. Goldsmith probably did not know that. He told how, from his window, he watched nesting rooks.

"I have often amused myself," he said, "with observing their plan of policy from my window in the Temple, that looks upon a grove, where they have made a colony in the midst of the City. At the commencement of Spring the rookery, which, during the continuance of Winter, seemed to have been deserted, or only guarded by five or six, like old soldiers in a garrison, now begins to be once more frequented; and in a short time all the bustle and hurry of business is fairly commenced."

All biographies of Goldsmith are written under the handicap of meagre information; and his conversational effervescence, being incomprehensible to Boswell, comes to us damped. With Johnson it is otherwise. Never was there a more fully documented life; and Johnson Societies keep regular meetings of remembrance. Many people suppose him to be the creator of Fleet Street. The magazine *Temple Bar* always bore on its mauve or cyclamen cover the motto "Sir, let us take a walk down Fleet Street—DOCTOR JOHNSON"; and he certainly, by his presence, dominated that part of the town. Horace Walpole called him the representative in epitome of all the contradictions in human nature; Gray, who likewise shuddered at that stubborn common sense, whispered (before Boswell did so) "Ursa Major." His walks, his frisks, his temperate visits with friends to taverns and coffee-houses, and his sometimes blustering but often generous conversational performances, are all familiar. Having been quoted, abused, ridiculed, and idolised for more than two hundred years, he is still, as a topic, unexhausted.

And yet in spite of his long and, in the eyes of the uninquiring, incessant association with Fleet Street, he did not live there all the time in his eventful half-century of London experience. When he came to town, fortified by the encouragement of an Irish painter met in Birmingham, who said he might manage on thirty pounds a year, lodge in a garret for eighteenpence a week, dine for sixpence, breakfast on bread and milk for a penny, and, by spending threepence in a coffee-house, enjoy good company for some hours every day, he found accommodation with Mr Norris, a stay-maker, in Exeter Street, Strand. "I dined very well," he said, remembering his Irish painter, "for eightpence, with very good company, at the Pineapple in New Street, just by." What else he did, in the matter of food and earning, is less well authenticated.

He then moved briefly to Greenwich, gaining experience which afterwards enabled him to retort effectively to the sallies of watermen. Later he was "up west," in both Woodstock Street, near Hanover Square, and Castle Street, Cavendish Square. It was from this second address that he issued his proposals for translating Father Paul Sarpi's *History of the Council of Trent*; and it was while here that he made acquaintance with Edward Cave, his friend and first bookseller-employer.

Either from the ups-and-downs of circumstance, or because he tired of his lodgings, or his landladies detested his idleness and untidiness, he went backwards and forwards between the Strand (at the Black Boy, over against Durham Court) and Bow Street, Fetter Lane and Holborn (where he lodged at the Golden Anchor); and it was not until he reached the house, No. 17 Gough Square, which is preserved as a shrine, that he settled within his proper domain. Carlyle, visiting the place nearly fifty years after Johnson's death, announced with disgust:

"We ourselves, not without labour and risk, lately discovered GOUGH SQUARE; and . . . the very House there, wherein the *English Dictionary* was composed. It is . . . a stout old fashioned, oak-balustraded house: 'I have spent many a pound and penny on it since then,' said the worthy landlord: 'Here, you see, this Bedroom was the Doctor's study; that was the garden' (a plot of delved ground somewhat larger than a bed-quilt), 'where he walked for exercise; these three garret Bedrooms' (where his three Copyists sat and wrote) 'were the place he kept his—*Pupils* in'! *Tempus edax rerum*! Yet *ferax* also: for our friend now added, with a wistful look, which strove to seem merely historical: 'I let it all in Lodgings to respectable gentlemen; by the quarter or the month; it's all one to me.'"

After his wife's death, Johnson made excursions to Staple Inn, Gray's Inn, and Inner Temple Lane. It was to Inner Temple Lane that Arthur Murphy was sent at the instigation of Wedderburn to offer him the pension of three hundred pounds a year which Horace Walpole found so distasteful. Murphy found it "an abode of wretchedness," and the author of *Rasselas* and the *English Dictionary* "in poverty, total illness, and the pride of literature." But Johnson took the pension, laughed at the outcry of those who declared that he had sold himself, and moved to Johnson's Court.

This Court was not named after him. He found it bearing that name; and he remained at No. 7 from 1765 for a dozen years. In 1777 he transferred himself to No. 8 Bolt Court, where he paid a rent of forty pounds a year; and he died in Bolt Court in 1784. No man ever loved London better than he did.

What of his friends, "the Johnson Circle"? There were some, very familiar as names to later generations, who were not always in his company, but who loved him well. Hogarth, for example, murmured "I'll tell you what; Sam Johnson's conversation is to the talk of other men like Titian's painting compared to Hudson's: but don't you tell people, now, that I say so; for the connoisseurs and I are at war, you

know; and because I hate *them*, they think I hate Titian—and let them!"
Hogarth, always at war with Reynolds, lived opposite to his innocent
but prosperous foe in Leicester Square. Reynolds had previously
lived in St Martin's Lane and Great Newport Street; and on the front
of the latter house, which nowadays is dazzlingly checkered, as well as
in Leicester Square, the fact of his residence is commemorated by a tablet.

Reynolds was a greater host than Johnson; his table was sometimes
so crowded that the casually and warmly invited guests had too little

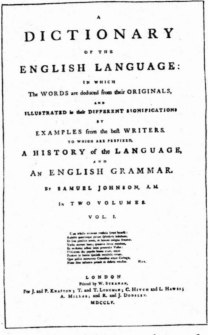

A

DICTIONARY

OF THE

ENGLISH LANGUAGE:

IN WHICH

The WORDS are deduced from their ORIGINALS,

AND

ILLUSTRATED in their DIFFERENT SIGNIFICATIONS

BY

EXAMPLES from the best WRITERS.

TO WHICH ARE PREFIXED,

A HISTORY of the LANGUAGE,

AND

AN ENGLISH GRAMMAR.

BY SAMUEL JOHNSON, A.M.

IN TWO VOLUMES.

VOL. I.

LONDON

Printed by W. STRAHAN,

For J. and P. KNAPTON; T. and T. LONGMAN; C. HITCH and L. HAWES;
A. MILLAR; and R. and J. DODSLEY.

MDCCLV.

Titlepage of the First Edition of
Johnson's *Dictionary* (1755)

to eat and not enough plates and glasses to go round. These deficiencies
greatly exasperated his youngest sister, Frances, who lived with him.
She was also exasperated because, she said, whenever any of Burke's
poor relations came to London they turned up, full of expectation, at
the Reynolds's table. However, her brother was not perturbed by
her exasperation; for he was a most equable man, and he liked company. It was at his table that Burke, Johnson, Goldsmith, and the rest
gathered as often as they gathered anywhere.

The circle included Dr Burney, Fox, Bennet Langton and Topham Beauclerk (two young gentlemen recently down from the University), Garrick, Percy, and Arthur Murphy. In a less strict sense it embraced almost everybody of intellectual note, and a few—but only a few—of the socially elect. Walpole and Gray, and of course their toady Mason, kept away. Chesterfield, having been savaged by Johnson, could hardly be expected to attend. The great political leaders had no longer any use for the friendship of writers and were immersed in warfare about the Court and the colonies. Only Fox and Burke, both brilliant House of Commons men, but Fox a gambler and member of the *ton*, while Burke "to party gave up what was meant for mankind," came to the famous gatherings. Therefore the names most familiar to us, apart from those of Burke and Fox and, once or twice, Wilkes, belonged to writers and artists, several of whom, such as Gibbon, were out of their element, while others are half-forgotten.

Of the celebrities, Burke was forced by his political allegiance—until he and his over-venturesome brothers bought the mansion and estate at Beaconsfield which was their home in spite of every impecuniosity—to reside in the West End. We therefore find him at different times in Dean's Yard, Westminster, in Lower Brook Street, and at Charles Street, St James's Square (this is the address to which, in 1781, the penniless young poet, George Crabbe, then lodging with a hairdresser in Bishopsgate, and rejected alike by Dodsley and Lord North, went by Burke's invitation, and came away on the high-road to fortune); at 37 Gerrard Street or in Duke Street, St James's. Fox also belonged, by birth as well as habit, to the West End. He was born in Conduit Street, and lived in both South Street and St James's Street. Whatever his gambling losses, he did not sink in the world. Walpole, passing along St James's Street one day, also in 1781, saw porters outside Fox's home loading coppers and old chests of drawers into a cart. The gossip ascertained that one of Fox's creditors, roused by news of his successes at faro, "actually seized and carried off his goods, which did not seem worth removing." Later that day the two men met; and Fox talked with what, to Walpole, was excessively irritating *sang froid*, as if nothing had happened.

Gibbon, a third visitant from drawing-rooms, was Putney-born. When, early in the seventeen-seventies, he went to live at 7 Bentinck Street, Westminster, he said he loved the dust of London, and felt he had "attained the first of earthly blessings, independence." But he had no chance of shining in the circle; and he really preferred the company of his friends Lord Sheffield and the Holroyds. He died in apartments in St James's Street, after having been "almost killed between Sheffield Place and East Grinstead, by hard, frozen, long and cross ruts, that would disgrace the approach of an Indian wigwam."

For the rest, Beauclerk and Langton were elegants, if not exquisites; they lived in the West. So did Boswell, who moved often, changing his apartments from penuriousness or because he was tired of his landlords. Sometimes he was in Downing Street, sometimes in Mayfair. Farington says he died in [Great] Tichfield Street. He was in Bolton Street, Piccadilly, when in 1769 he gave his historic dinner to Johnson, Reynolds, Goldsmith and Garrick. The extraordinary young host, so stingy towards prostitutes, so lickspittle to every notability, so jealous of all who were praised by Johnson, and yet so gifted in the arts of ingratiation and dramatic memory, gleamed in triumph at such a gathering of the famous at his table. "London," he said, "is undoubtedly a place where men and manners may be seen to the greatest advantage. The liberty and whim that reigns there occasions a variety of perfect and curious characters." Boswell himself was not the least curious among these perfect characters.

Another who was very curious was Nollekens, the sculptor, of whom Johnson was very fond. We only know of the Nollekens ménage from a prejudiced witness. J. T. Smith, who, disappointed of a fortune from his master, became his malicious biographer, gives a hundred glimpses of the dirt and stinginess of an eccentric genius, big-headed, short in the body ("which was too large, particularly in the front lower part"), whose bow legs resembled his hooked nose, which in turn resembled the rudder of an Antwerp packet-boat. Nollekens, born in Soho, lived the whole of his married life at No. 9 Mortimer Street, Cavendish Square. He was much given to answering the door himself, which Smith thought a "vulgar" habit; and when making a bust of Johnson he greeted the sitter, who had arrived late, with the whine "Now, Doctor, you *did* say you would give my busto half an hour before dinner, and the dinner has been waiting this long time." Dr Johnson's impenitent answer was "Bow-wow-wow."

Hazlitt has a beautiful sketch in an essay called *The Old Age of Artists* of Nollekens talking with James Northcote; and Northcote, who was one of Reynolds's pupils, and lived alarmedly to lament the publication of Hazlitt's *Conversations* with himself in 1830, represents a noteworthy bridge between the eighteenth and nineteenth centuries.

Northcote does not mention—nor does Hazlitt—two other men of whimsical interest to modern readers. The first of these was Dr John Hawkesworth, who collaborated with and imitated Johnson in periodical essays entitled *The Adventurer*; and who wrote a too-fanciful account of Captain Cook's voyages. For this latter work, which was freely based on Cook's Journals, he received six thousand pounds; but he was disowned by Cook; and, being thereupon hounded for rapacity and incompetence by every unsuccessful scribbler of the seventeen-seventies, sank under persecution. He was a serious man, formal in conversation, rather ignorant, very over-literary, and nowadays unreadable. His home was in Lime Street, in the City; and there he died of indignant shame with his six thousand pounds unspent.

A less excusable associate of Johnson's was Sir John Hawkins, the magistrate and author of a History of Music. Hawkins must have been easily the least popular member of the circle, and I do not think anybody ever understood why he was made Johnson's executor. He took advantage of his position to write the first biography of Johnson, which would be forgotten if it had not been so roughly handled by Boswell. This was the man described to Burney by Johnson as "very unclubbable." "Yet I really believe him," added Johnson, "to be an honest man at the bottom; though to be sure he is rather penurious, and somewhat mean, and it must be owned he has some degree of brutality, and is not without a tendency to savageness that cannot well be defended." Hawkins lived and died in a house by the Broad Sanctuary, Westminster.

Johnson's rich benefactor, Henry Thrale, the brewer, whose country house was at Streatham, lived at Deadman's Place, Southwark, near his brewery. Under advice from doctors, he moved to Grosvenor Square, where he died. His widow, who afterwards did not spare Johnson for his disapproval of her second marriage, took a house in Welbeck Street when she became Mrs Piozzi; but she soon went to Italy with her new husband, "the great Italian singer," whom she "picked up" (her own words) at Brighton in 1780; and it was in Florence that she wrote her hostile, self-excusing, and underrated *Anecdotes of the late Samuel Johnson*.

Dr Burney, father of Fanny, used to go to the Thrales' house at Streatham to give piano lessons to their eldest daughter, Esther, or Queeny; and he there became intimate with Johnson. He lived for perhaps ten years with his family in Poland Street, and Fanny at least, calling it "dear Poland Street," left that address with reluctance. It was exchanged in 1770 for Queen's Square, where the Burneys had "a charming house . . . situated at the upper end of the square," with "a delightful prospect of Hamsted and Hygate." Dr Burney liked this house because John Barber, the "Johannes Tonsor" of Swift and his friends, had lived in it. But John Barber could not compare in importance with Isaac Newton; and Burney, a snob, ever-conscious of his lowly surroundings in childhood, rejoiced when, four years later, he took possession of the house in St Martin's Street, Leicester Square, which had formerly belonged to Newton.

This was No. 1 in the Street—"an odious Street," Fanny called it—later described in the biography of Nollekens as being No. 36, "next door to Orange Street Chapel."

Burney had been unwell, and was staying in the country; but the moment he could travel Fanny wrote in her diary (October 18th, 1774) that

"We came immediately to this house, which we propose calling *Newton House*, or *The Observatory*, or something that sounds *grand*. By the way Sir Isaac's identical observatory is still subsisting, and we show it, to all our visitors, as our principal Lyon."

The observatory, which Fanny used for reading and meditation, "overlooked all London and its environs." It was a glazed turret, with a small fireplace and cupboard; and as it consisted solely of miniature panes of glass united by a flimsy framework, it was soon largely blown away by a hurricane.

The last of Johnson's friends whom I shall mention is Samuel Richardson, son of a joiner who migrated for safety to Derbyshire on the fall of his patron, the Duke of Monmouth. Samuel was apprenticed to a printer. His own story, that he used as a boy of thirteen to write their love-letters for illiterate girls, is unimpeachable; and those —how many are there, nowadays, I wonder?—who read *Clarissa* will understand one of these girls who said, "I cannot tell you what to write; but (her heart on her lips) you cannot write too kindly." This was the germ of his later wisdom, and of the epistolary and psychological novel. Richardson was very shrewd. Having gained experience as a journeyman printer he started in business on his own account just off Fleet Street. There, besides printing, he compiled indexes, wrote introductions, and concocted what he called "honest dedications." He prospered.

He prospered so well that after writing an educational work called

Familiar Letters to and from several Persons upon Business and Other Subjects, and his three great novels, he engaged in 1755 in building not only splendid new printing premises in Salisbury Square, but (in place of their country home at North End, west of Kensington) a fine residence at Parsons Green. "Everybody," he complacently said, when it was too late for any further change, "is more pleased with what I have done than my wife."

Samuel Richardson

Whether Mrs Richardson disliked the move from North End is not revealed; but the Richardson home there, about a mile beyond Holland House and "well on the road to Richmond and Twickenham," was long afterwards greatly to the taste of Angela Thirkell, when that delightful author was a child.

"In the summer of 1751, (says Mrs Thirkell, in *Three Houses*) Samuel Richardson invited a party of friends to his country house at North End to hear a reading of the manuscript of *Sir Charles Grandison* in the grotto. . . . Richardson died in 1761 and his world departed. But the house with the grotto remained, the mulberry tree in the garden grew and spread, and more than a hundred years after his death a poet and a painter, walking on a Sunday afternoon by fields and lanes from Kensington, saw it and were strongly attracted to it as it stood tenantless. The poet was William Allingham. . . . The painter was Edward Burne-Jones. . . . North End Lane was a shabby enough thoroughfare at its northern end, but as one walked down it the little houses and shops soon came to an end and there were prosperous, comely, red-brick houses of Queen Anne's time, each standing in its own garden with fields behind."

One of these houses, ruined then by stucco, was Richardson's. It contained a room of the ideal size for a studio; and Burne-Jones lived there from the year 1867.

7 *The Romantics; Charles and Mary Lamb; Crabb Robinson; Hazlitt; Coleridge*

That is an instance of the continuity of the arts which delights me, as I hope it delights you. And I like to remember also that as the eighteenth century drew to a close, when Cowper and Crabbe, Bowles and Blake were making their so different contributions to English literature, other men were already alive who were to carry that literature into a new coloured phase of its history.

While Johnson and his friends gathered and talked in what might be called the Old World, new worlds had arisen, just as they have done in our own day. Voltaire and Rousseau—the one full of admiration, the other of suspicion—had visited England; Benjamin Franklin, formerly a printer in Bartholomew Close and Lincoln's Inn Fields, had dabbled in letters to inconvenient purpose; and revolution was in the air. Indeed, both Chesterfield and Goldsmith had remarked it in prophetic terms; the former by saying, in December, 1753, "all the symptoms, which I have ever met with in history, previous to great changes and revolutions in government, now exist, and daily increase, in France." The revolutions had arrived during the childhood or boyhood of the new generation, which grew up in an England already heaving against excess of authority.

Johnson, dismissing Rousseau's paradoxes as expressions of the passion for novelty, did not die until 1784; Boswell not until 1795. But Wordsworth was born in 1770, Scott in 1771, Coleridge in 1772, Southey in 1774, Lamb in 1775, Hazlitt in 1778, Leigh Hunt in 1784, and De Quincey in 1785. Thus, although they were the new generation, their social and intellectual background was that of the eighteenth century. All, in the matter of philosophy, were filled with debate over Hartley's doctrine (let me be more exact: elaboration of a doctrine which Hume also had canvassed) of "the association of ideas," and, in the matter of poetry, over the sonnets of Bowles. All were trying not only to reconcile deep religious faith with physical science, but to establish whole new social and metaphysical systems. At the same time they were feeling their way back to ecstasy through such poetical literature as was immediately at hand.

Something else can be observed, too. It is a recovery of quick romantic observation of the scene before their eyes. Lamb was a Londoner—the only one of those I have named who was born in this city;—and you must contrast his picture of his surroundings under the Regency with what had been written a hundred years before by Ward or Gay.

"The lighted shops of the Strand and Fleet Street," says Lamb; " the innumerable trades, tradesmen, and customers, coaches, waggons, playhouses; all the bustle and wickedness round about Covent Garden; the very women of the Town; the watchmen, drunken scenes, rattles;—life awake, if you awake, at all hours of the night; the crowds, the very dirt and mud, the sun shining upon houses and pavements; the print-shops, the old book-stalls, parsons cheapening books, coffee-houses, steams of soups from kitchens, the pantomimes—London itself a pantomime and a masquerade— all these things work themselves into my mind, and feed me, without a power of satiating me."

Have you otherwise heard such language? Does not Lamb but expand the enthusiasm of Sam Johnson, nay, of Ben Jonson and Dekker? Does he not speak in the accent of Dickens? Well did Oliver Goldsmith say that "eloquence is not in the words, but in the subject." "These things work themselves into my mind, and feed me."

There had been few such Londoners as Lamb since the Elizabethan days. "I was born," he says, "and passed the first seven years of my life, in the Temple. Its church, its halls, its gardens, its fountains, its river, I had almost said—for in those young years, what was this king of rivers to me but a stream that watered our pleasant places?—these are my oldest recollections." He was born in the Temple. He went to school at Christ's Hospital when it was in Newgate Street, and when the school, according to the headmaster, was father, mother, brother, sister, first and second cousin, and every other relation the pupil might require. He worked at the South Sea House when it was "a melancholy-looking, handsome, brick and stone edifice, where Threadneedle Street abuts upon Bishopsgate." And, apart from visits to Hertfordshire in childhood and to the Lakes and elsewhere to see his friends, he remained within the easiest reach of central London until 1827, when he went to Enfield, to "the prettiest, compactest house I ever saw."

Most of Lamb's homes were described in superlatives which perhaps they did not deserve. The fact shows his contented mind; and

ELIA   *From the sketch by Maclise in the Dyce & Forster Collection*

Charles Lamb, from a sketch by Maclise

as long as his sister was well they stayed happily for long periods in whatever lodging they had. In the first-recorded of these lodgings, at 7 Little Queen Street, Holborn, Mary frantically stabbed her invalid mother to the heart. She would then have been kept in an asylum for life if Charles had not sworn to guard her as long as he himself lived. As it was, he and his father moved away from the fatal house; the father died; and by 1800 Charles and Mary, alone, were at No. 45

Chapel Street, Pentonville, between King's Cross and Upper Street, Islington. From 1801 until 1809 they lived at No. 16 Mitre Court Buildings, in

> "delectable rooms, which look out (when you stand a tip-toe) over the Thames and Surrey Hills; at the upper end of King's Bench Walks, in the Temple . . . I shall be as airy, up four pair of stairs, as in the country; and in a garden, in the midst of enchanting (more than Mahometan paradise) London, whose dirtiest drab-frequented alley, and her lowest bowing tradesman, I would not exchange for Skiddaw, Helvellyn, etc. O her lamps of a night! her rich gold-smiths, print-shops, toy-shops, mercers, hardwaremen, pastry-cooks, St Paul's Churchyard, the Strand, Exeter Change, Charing Cross, with the man *upon* a black horse! These are thy gods, O London! . . . All the streets and pavements are pure gold, I warrant you. At least, I know an alchemy that turns her mud into that metal—a mind that loves to be at home in crowds."

Alas, this paradise was not to be eternal; and in 1809 the landlord claimed it for himself. But Lamb endured the disaster. He stayed for a little while at 34 Southampton Buildings, where Hazlitt had been two years before, and where Coleridge followed in 1811; and then he found "far more commodious and roomy" accommodation at No. 4 Inner Temple Lane, overlooking Hare Court.

> " I have two sitting-rooms; I call them so *par excellence*, for you may stand, or loll, or lean, or try any posture in them, but they are best for sitting . . . I have two of these rooms on the third floor, and five sleeping, cooking etc. rooms, on the fourth floor. In my best room is a choice collection of the works of Hogarth, an English painter of some humour. In my next best are shelves containing a small but well-chosen library. My best room commands a court, in which there are trees and a pump, the water of which is excellent cold, with brandy, and not very insipid without."

Crabb Robinson, never as effervescent as Lamb, described this wonderful residence as "a garret"; which shows that when our an-cestors used that term they did not always mean a cupboard under the tiles.

Lamb was at Inner Temple Lane for six years, after which he lodged with Mr Owens, an ironmonger, at No. 20 Russell Court, Covent Garden East. This place was "a little noisy," but "delightfully situated between the two theatres" (Drury Lane and Covent Garden), and it suited Charles and Mary, who did not move again until 1823. Then they went to another perfect abode, a cottage in Colebrooke Row, Islington:

"a white house with six good rooms; the New River (rather elderly by this time) runs (if a modest walking pace can be so termed) close to the foot of the house; and behind is a spacious garden, with vines (I assure you), pears, strawberries, parsnips, leeks, carrots, cabbages, to delight the heart of old Alcinous. You enter without passage into a cheerful dining-room, all studded over and rough with old Books, and above is a lightsome Drawing-room, three windows, full of choice prints. I feel like a great Lord."

Here Mary showed Crabb Robinson her brother's books, "the finest collection of shabby books I ever saw; such a number of first-rate works in very shabby condition is, I think, nowhere to be found." And, within a stone's throw, also in Colebrooke Row, lived for a time Robert Southey, Poet Laureate, third and last of the Lake Poets, and virulent reviewer, but still Lamb's friend.

It was at Inner Temple Lane that Crabb Robinson first met Wordsworth; for Lamb gathered all men to him and made them feel at home. Whether it was Wordsworth or Coleridge, Hazlitt or Godwin, Leigh Hunt or George Dyer, the eccentric who managed to fall into the New River, or those various Quakers (the Bartons and the Lloyds) with whom he maintained such constant friendship, or Fanny Burney's brothers, or James White, the author of *The Letters of Sir John Falstaff*, everybody of clear intelligence who had a heart to share and a foot in London turned thither.

Crabb Robinson, prodigious talker and walker, who later helped to found London University, records many visits.

"I went late to Lamb's. His party were there, and a numerous and odd set they were;—for the most part interesting and amusing people— George Dyer, Captain and Martin Burney, Ayrton, Phillips, Hazlitt and wife, Alsager, Barron Field, Coulson, John Collier, Talfourd, White, Lloyd and Basil Montagu.

"Southey had been with Blake, and admired both his designs and his poetic talents. At the same time he held him to be a decided madman. Blake, he said, spoke of his visions with the diffidence which is usual with such people, and did not seem to expect that he should be believed. He showed Southey a perfectly mad poem, called 'Jerusalem.' Oxford Street is in Jerusalem."

"At C. Lamb's. Coleridge there. A short but interesting conversation on German metaphysics.

"Tea with the Lambs. Hazlitt there, much depressed.

"Went to Lamb's, found the Wordsworths there, and having walked with them to Westminster Bridge, returned to Lamb's, and sat an hour with Macready, a very pleasing man, gentlemanly in his manners, and sensible and well informed."

Most of the visitors were sensible and well-informed. They came, not, as Johnson's visitors did, to hear a bow-wow-wow talker, but to talk themselves. It was understood that Lamb and his sister could not often—because of the latter's health—go out; and the generation which sought the Mitre or the Turk's Head was gone. There were still coffee-houses; Hazlitt long frequented one at the Chancery Lane end of Southampton Buildings, which he made the scene of his essay on *Coffee House Politicians*. But the Lamb circle preferred a domestic setting. Authors were not yet quite family men; but they were moving towards Victorian ways, and Lamb, having a sister and an earned competence, could welcome them all. Of strangers, it was not asked, Hazlitt said, "had they written anything?" for wit and good-fellowship were alone desiderated, and nobody but the insipid, the affected, and the fine gentleman was shunned.

Those who came, talked. They talked, chiefly, of literature, because books were Lamb's passion. And, says Hazlitt,

"when a set of adepts, of *illuminati*, get about a question, it is worth while to hear them talk. They may snarl and quarrel over it, like dogs; but they pick it bare to the bone. . . . We used to have many lively skirmishes at the Thursday evening parties. . . . There was Lamb himself, the most delightful, the most provoking, the most witty and sensible of men. He always made the best pun, and the best remark in the course of the evening. His serious conversation, like his serious writing, is his best. No one ever stammered out such fine, piquant, deep, eloquent things in half a dozen half-sentences as he does. . . . How often did we cut into the haunch of letters, while we discussed the haunch of mutton on the table! How we skimmed the cream of criticism! How we got into the heart of controversy! How we picked out the marrow of authors!"

Hazlitt picked out, not only the marrow, but the hearts and livers of the authors he arraigned for tamed radical zeal; and therefore he and Southey and Wordsworth were never on the best of terms. But Lamb loved everybody, and everybody who came felt himself a free man. He quarrelled, if at all, on the question whether this government or the last was the worse. The group was a democracy in which all men were, or had been, radicals.

It always interests me to know what famous men were like; and I hope it is the same with you. We have many pen-portraits of them. Coleridge, said De Quincey,

> "might seem to be about five feet eight (he was, in reality, about an inch and a half taller, but his figure was of an order which drowns the height); his person was broad and full, and tended even to corpulence; his complexion was fair, though not what painters technically style fair, because it was associated with black hair; his eyes were large, and soft in their expression; and it was from the peculiar appearance of haze or dreaminess which mixed with their light that I recognised him."

> "Brow and head were round," said Carlyle, more severely, speaking of a Coleridge who had left the Lakes and taken refuge for life with Mr Gilman, an apothecary, at Highgate; "and of massive weight, but the face was flabby and irresolute. The deep eyes, of a light hazel, were as full of sorrow as of inspiration; confused pain looked mildly from them, as in a kind of mild astonishment. The whole figure and air, good and amiable otherwise, might be called flabby . . . . His voice, naturally soft and good, had contracted itself into a plaintive snuffle and singsong. . . . I still recollect his 'object' and 'subject', terms of continual recurrence in the Kantean province; and how he sung and snuffled them into 'om-m-mject' and 'sum-m-mject'," with a kind of solemn shake or quaver as he rolled along. No talk, in this century or in any other, could be more surprising."

Carlyle was always harsh in his estimates, and this one is less adverse than his early sketch of Lamb himself, as a "pitiful, rickety, gasping, staggering, stammering Tomfool," "in some considerable degree insane," and "a confirmed, shameless drunkard." Furthermore, the Coleridge he saw was "now getting old, towards sixty perhaps." The snuffle was less noticeable at Lamb's, where Coleridge was only famous for brilliant, inexhaustible monologue.

Wordsworth distributed his company, once had lodgings near Cavendish Square, and stayed sometimes with a friend in Gloucester

Place, sometimes at "Old Mrs Hoare's" at Hampstead. This last, a Quaker home, is the place where Caroline Fox, also a charming Quaker with whom Carlyle's friend, John Sterling, was in love, met him.

"He is a man (she said) of middle height and not of very striking appearance, the lower part of his face retreating a little, his eye of somewhat French diplomatic character, with heavy eyelids, and none of the flashing which one connects with poetic genius. When speaking earnestly his manner and voice become extremely energetic; and the peculiar emphasis, and even accent, he throws into some of his words add considerably to their force. He evidently loves the monologue style of conversation, but shows great candour in giving due consideration to any remarks which others may make."

One has the—apparently erroneous—impression that Wordsworth talked only and incessantly of his own poetry, which he said nobody, not even Coleridge, quite understood. Coleridge was not happy enough to understand it. "No man who lives a life of constant bustle, and whose felicity depends on the opinions of others, can possibly comprehend the best of my poems." "I am myself one of the happiest of men." No wonder Keats spoke of "the Wordsworthian or egotistical sublime"!

As for Hazlitt, he was, says Patmore,

"a pale anatomy of a man, sitting uneasily, half on half off a chair, with his legs tucked awkwardly underneath the rail, his hands folded listlessly on his knees, his head drooping on one side, and one of his elbows leaning (not resting) on the edge of the table . . . as if in fear of its having no right to be there. His eyes were not good. There was a furtive and at times a sinister look about them, as they glanced suspiciously from under their overhanging brows . . . . Hazlitt entered a room as if he had been brought to it in custody; he shuffled sidelong to the nearest chair, sat himself down upon one corner of it, dropped his hat and his eyes upon the floor . . . and seemed to resign himself to his fate."

I hope he did not do this at Lamb's! Such an entry would not only have affronted his host; it would have belied his enjoyment of the best company then to be had in London.

8 *Radicalism; Godwin; Shelley; Leigh Hunt; Keats; Haydon*

There were no lords in the Lamb circle. Most of its members were of comparatively small means and undistinguished birth. Few of them had been to a University. If they had not been geniuses, they would have been very small fry in the world. That is why Lamb for so long, not having met him, felt animosity to Tom Moore, a great diner-out and frequenter of Society, who never lodged farther east than Bury Street, St James's, or Davies Street, Berkeley Square. That is why Rogers, the banker-poet, who once, in youth, ran away after knocking at Dr Johnson's door, and who lived and died in St James's Place, did not go to Inner Temple Lane or Russell Street. Lord Byron did not go; Sir Walter Scott, being a Tory, got no nearer than Northcote's, where he sat to the painter; and even Sydney Smith, a strong Whig, founder of the *Edinburgh Review*, for which Hazlitt worked, and a man of the greatest humanity, might hardly have heard of the Lambs (he made an ignorant *mot* about Lamb's beer-drinking) nor been heard of by them.

They belonged to the tyrant-hating Radicals; and the tyrant-hating Radicals were suspect. It did not matter that Charles and Mary were peaceful lovers of poetry and prose (Mary proudly remembered having as a child seen Goldsmith in the Temple); nor that, in politics, their friends were emotional but innocuous. The Monarchy was vulnerably shady. Governments, observing the state of France, and vexed by Jacobins and Chartists at home, were alarmed into repression. The political weather accordingly looked harsh to the Lamb group, which, having never heard that escapism was an unheroic vice, and having newly discovered for itself the glories of Elizabethan drama and the sublimities of seventeenth and eighteenth century pietists, from Vaughan and Herbert to John Woolman, preferred the world of spirit to the world of Canning and Castlereagh.

Godwin was the eldest of this group, born as early as 1756. He was believed by Shelley (absorbed in "his daedal rounds with nature, and his Archimedean endeavours to move the globe with his own hands") to be dead and immortal until, one day in 1813, the poet went visiting and found in the room "a short, stout, thickset old man, with a very fair complexion, and with a bald and very large head," whose appearance "was altogether that of a dissenting minister," and who rapidly became, as he remained for several years, a thorn in Shelley's flesh.

I do not enlarge on the fact that intellectual revolutionaries always look mild; but remark that Shelley's descriptions showed insight. Godwin as a young man had in fact attended the Dissenting College in Hoxton; and in pursuing political justice to its logical but not altogether reasonable ends he dissented from most men, including himself. He was in the course of his long life a rationalist philosopher, historian, biographer, pamphleteer (for he at one time sensationally and effectively revived the pamphlet as an instrument of protest), novelist,

William Godwin : A Caricature

playwright, publisher, and composer of books for children. He was also a talker. Hazlitt said that when other men talked Godwin fell asleep, and that when Godwin talked the other men slept.

He was always, not entirely by his own fault, short of money, for which he had no head; and posterity knows him less as a philosopher than as a wide and persistent borrower. This shortage of money may account for many of his changes of address, from Cripplegate to Holborn; the Strand; Chalton Street, Somers Town, behind Euston

Road (here he wrote most of *Caleb Williams,* his best novel); the Polygon, Clarendon Square, Somers Town (where as he sunned himself on a balcony the future second Mrs Godwin, a virago disguised in green spectacles, interrupted him with the ominous inquiry "Is it possible that I behold the immortal Godwin?"); Hanway Street, Oxford Street, the scene of his first venture into publishing; larger premises at 41 Skinner Street, which stood where Snow Hill stands today; 195 Strand; and 44 Gower Place. As a philosopher he is due for revival; as a publisher of children's books he was associated with the Lambs' *Tales from Shakespeare, Mrs Leicester's School,* and other small works, together with a grammar for children by Hazlitt and many books of his own; as a novelist he is bad but historically interesting; and as a man, in spite of all inconvenient habits, he was liked and made pleasant fun of. Lamb once gave him fifty ill-spared pounds.

Shelley, an aristocrat who took his eager philosophy almost entire from Godwin, was really outside the circle; he published *Queen Mab* from 23 Chapel Street, Grosvenor Square, and in early days was for a time at 15 Poland Street; otherwise his visits were sporadic. But Leigh Hunt was in it, and Leigh Hunt went to prison for calling the Prince Regent "a corpulent Adonis." He served an agreeable two years' sentence in the Surrey Gaol, turning one of the infirmary wards

"into a noble room. I papered the walls with a trellis of roses; I had the ceiling coloured with clouds and sky; the barred windows I screened with Venetian blinds; and when my bookcases were set up with their busts, and flowers and a pianoforte made their appearance, perhaps there was not a handsomer room on that side the water. I took a pleasure, when a stranger knocked at the door, to see him come in and stare about him. The surprise on issuing from the Borough, and passing through the avenues of a gaol, was dramatic. Charles Lamb declared there was no other such room, except in a fairy tale."

Hunt was visited by many friends and admirers, including Hazlitt and Lord Byron, who brought Tom Moore; and as he had extraordinary charm of manner everything was as easy as grace itself. "He was rather tall," said his son, "as straight as an arrow, and looked slenderer than he really was. His hair was black and shining, and slightly inclined to wave; his head was high, his forehead straight and white, his eyes black and sparkling." But he had no command of money. He was not as hard-up as Godwin or another member of the circle,

Haydon the painter, who was maddened by ambition and bankruptcy; but so hard-up that the stories of his spongings on Carlyle and others, which culminate in Dickens's not very subtle caricature of Harold Skimpole, are pleasanter than those of the other man's extremity only because they are less desperate. He worked hard; he was gay; his wife over-spent; life became less a reality than an exercise in fancy. Only when Lord John Russell, with what John Forster called "eccentrically statesmanlike attention to literature," gave him a Civil List Pension of two hundred pounds a year did it become almost unnecessary for his friends to support him.

Hunt was born in Southgate in 1784, went to Christ's Hospital, and for a time was simultaneously a clerk in the War Office and a dramatic critic. In 1808 he established, with his brother John, the often-execrated Radical periodical *The Examiner*; and it was in *The Examiner* that he libelled the Regent. When imprisonment ceased, he went to live in Edgware Road, where Byron continued to visit him and where Wordsworth also came; but in 1816, for the sake of the seven sorts of air which Mrs Nollekens thought the district must enjoy, he moved to Hampstead. Here he had a cottage in that Vale of Health which Mrs Nollekens called "a stagnate bottom, a pit in the heath, where if a bit of paper is whirling in the air, it can never rise above the high ground about it." To this cottage came both Shelley and Keats.

Hunt himself said it was not at Hampstead that he first saw Keats.

"It was in York Buildings, in the New (Marylebone) Road (No. 8), where I wrote part of the *Indicator*—and he resided with me while in Mortimer Terrace, Kentish Town (No. 13), where I concluded it. I mention this for the curious in such things; among whom I am one."

I hope that we are all curious (and more accurate) in such things; as in Hunt's next move, which was nothing less than the transport of his entire family to Italy at the invitation of Byron. There, in time, he began to write those articles for *The Examiner* which were the first slight sketches for *The Town*. They made him homesick.

"When I put on my cap, and pitched myself in imagination into the thick of Covent Garden, the pleasure I received was so vivid —I turned the corner of a street so much in the ordinary course of things, and was so tangibly present to the pavement, the shop-windows, the people, and a thousand agreeable recollections which looked me naturally in the face, that sometimes when I walk there now, the impression hardly seems more real. I used to feel as if I actually pitched my soul there, and that spiritual eyes might have seen it shot over from Tuscany into York Street, like a rocket."

He returned to England in 1825, and went to Highgate, near the house where Coleridge lived with Mr Gilman; left Highgate before Coleridge's death; stayed briefly at Epsom; "in a sequestered corner of Old Brompton"; and in St John's Wood; and in 1833 went to live in Upper Cheyne Row, Chelsea, where the Carlyles were near neighbours. He moved again in 1840, to Kensington; and in 1853 to a cottage in Hammersmith, the last of his abiding-places.

Like the rest of his contemporaries, Hunt was a great talker, "apt," Hazlitt said, "to put people to their trumps."

"He sits at the head of a party with great gaiety and grace; has an elegant manner and turn of features; . . . has continual sportive sallies of wit or fancy; tells a story capitally; mimics an actor, or an acquaintance to admiration; laughs with great glee and good humour at his own or other people's jokes; understands the point of an equivoke, or an observation immediately; has a taste and knowledge of books, of music, of medals; manages an argument adroitly; is genteel and gallant, and has a set of by-phrases and quaint allusions always at hand to produce a laugh."

No wonder such a man, his senior by eleven years, and much more conversant with the world, should have fascinated the twenty-one-year-old John Keats. Keats, the son of a young ostler who had married his employer's daughter, had been born over the livery stables at the sign of the Swan and Hoop, Finsbury Pavement. His parents died early; and he and his brothers then lived with their maternal grandmother in Church Street, Edmonton. He was sent to a good school at Enfield, and was later apprenticed to an Edmonton surgeon. This apprenticeship was cancelled; when he was eighteen Keats left home to attend students' classes at Guy's and St Thomas's Hospitals.

At first, he lodged alone at 8 Dean Street, in the Borough; afterwards he joined fellow-students in lodgings in St Thomas's Street in the same district. Dickens knew that neighbourhood well five or six years later; and has left a picture of Lant Street, where Bob Sawyer lodged, which will bring it to our eyes:

"The majority of the inhabitants either direct their energies to the letting of furnished apartments, or devote themselves to the healthful and invigorating pursuit of mangling. The chief features in the still life of the street are green shutters; lodging-bills, brass door-plates, and bell-handles; the principal specimens of animated nature, the pot-boy, the muffin youth, and the baked-potato man. The population is migratory, usually disappearing on the verge of quarter day, and generally by night. His Majesty's revenues are seldom collected in this happy valley; the rents are dubious; and the water communication is very frequently cut off."

However, in 1816 Keats joined his brothers in lodgings in the Poultry, over a passage leading to the Queen's Head tavern; and it was about this time that, after some of his work had been shown to Horace Smith and Leigh Hunt, the meeting with Hunt took place at Hampstead. For a year longer the brothers were at 76 Cheapside; after which, in 1817, they went to Hampstead, to a house in Well Walk kept by some people named Bentley. Either in these apartments or in the house of his new friend Charles Brown, in what was then called Wentworth Place (it has become Keats Grove), Keats lived, with excursions far and near in search of health or solitude, until that terrible day when he recognised that he had coughed arterial blood. For a few weeks after this, in 1820, he was in Wesleyan Place, Kentish Town, in order to be near Hunt; then he stayed with the Hunts, to be nursed, in Mortimer Street, close by. But in September, 1820, he sailed from London to Italy, and died in Rome in February, 1821.

Keats had good friends, from Joseph Severn, the Hoxton-born Royal Academy Gold Medallist, who was beside him at the end, to John Hamilton Reynolds, Charles Cowden Clarke, Dilke, and Brown. Those friends whose names have survived for reasons other than their friendship for Keats were unquestionably Leigh Hunt and Benjamin Robert Haydon. Hunt we have met; Haydon, that zealot for historical painting, the Elgin Marbles, size, and fresco, must be briefly mentioned, less for his painting (which is outside the scope of this book) than for his sensationally dramatic autobiography.

He came from Devonshire in 1804, at the age of eighteen, to lodgings which had been taken for him at 342 Strand. He had an introduction to James Northcote, then living in 39 Argyll Street, between Great Marlborough Street and Regent Street (but afterwards at No. 8 Argyll Place, where Hazlitt noted his *Conversations* and Scott, who thought he resembled an animated mummy, sat for a portrait); and found Northcote "a diminutive wizened figure in an old blue striped dressing-gown, his spectacles pushed up on his forehead." Northcote was rightly discouraging; but Haydon, buoyed by a fever of optimistic egotism, pooh-poohed the discouragement, and ecstatically cried "Hurrah for dear old London—hurrah!"

Still buoyant, Haydon "moved more to the West end, as better for health," and lodged at 3 Broad Street (Blake was born at No. 28), Carnaby Market, near Great Marlborough Street. He had not then been incommoded by ill-health.

"So far from the smoke of London being offensive to me, it has always been to my imagination the sublime canopy that shrouds the City of the World. Drifted by the wind or hanging in gloomy grandeur over the vastness of our Babylon, the sight of it always filled my mind with feelings of energy such as no other spectacle could inspire. 'Be Gode,' said Fuseli to me one day, 'it's like de smoke of de Israelites making bricks.' 'It is grander,' said I, 'for it is the smoke of a people who would have made the Egyptians make bricks for them.' 'Well done, John Bull,' replied Fuseli."

After his mother's death, in 1808, Haydon found first-floor accommodation at 41 Great Marlborough Street. Alas! he suffered many disappointments; fell hundreds of pounds in arrears with his rent; and had to part with clothes, watch, and books. His landlord and landlady anxiously tended him; and when he had a stroke of luck he paid them two hundred pounds on account of his arrears and allowed them to draw a bill for the balance. As he became involved in artistic controversy he could earn nothing, went to moneylenders, could not repay his borrowings; passed from bad to worse; and at last collapsed from starvation. Still seeking better air, he left Great Marlborough Street, took lodgings at Somers Town, and in a short time went to live at 22 Lisson Grove North, as tenant to a Royal Academician named Rossi.

It was at Lisson Grove that he gave the "immortal dinner" at which he introduced Keats to Wordsworth and completed the party with Lamb and Monkhouse. He was intoxicated with triumph and brilliant hopes. But he could not pay his rent. Four years later he was arrested at the instance of no fewer than a hundred and fifty creditors (including his landlord and his colourman). By some miracle of personality he escaped being made a bankrupt. Somehow he managed to rent a house, this time in Connaught Terrace. Arrest followed arrest; appeal, appeal; disaster, disaster; and his own buoyancy and the prodigious generosity of many kinds of men, from Sir Robert Peel and Sir Walter Scott to his landlord, W. F. Newton, enabled him to carry on month after month; until at last, distraught by a realisation that he never could overcome his difficulties, he committed suicide, in the sixty-first year of his age, 1846, nine years after Queen Victoria's accession. He had lived in four reigns. He left a wife and children, and a number of unsold and unsaleable paintings. He owed three thousand pounds. And among the provisions of his will was one by which all his manuscripts and personal memoirs became the property of Miss Barrett, of 50 Wimpole Street.

9 Dickens; change in the literary situation; Sydney Smith; St John's Wood; George Eliot

You realise what—in the matter of time—this means. Haydon and Leigh Hunt had both known intimately such a man as Godwin, who was middle-aged at the turn of the century. They had belonged to a group whose early ideas of poetry and philosophy had been dominated by eighteenth-century theory and practice. They now lived in a world to which the eighteenth century was archaic. By 1846, when Haydon died, Dickens was thirty-eight, and had already passed from *The Pickwick Papers* to *Martin Chuzzlewit* and *A Christmas Carol*. He had spent his childhood in Bayham Street, Camden Town; at No. 4 Gower Street; in Little College Street; in Somers Town; and, by stages, at Hampstead; in Seymour Street; Bentinck Street, Manchester Square; etc. He had occupied rooms in Furnival's Inn, and, having married, had spent a couple of years in the famous 48 Doughty Street house, and had moved out of it in 1839 into No. 1 Devonshire Terrace, Marylebone, where he had "a handsome house with a garden of considerable size, shut out from the New Road by a high brick wall facing the York gate into Regent's Park"; and there he wrote *David Copperfield*, which began to appear in parts early in 1849.

Thackeray at the end of 1846 was on the staff of *Punch*, was considering the theme of *Vanity Fair*, which began publication early in the following year, and was settled comfortably in Young Street, Kensington. He had lived at 13 Great Coram Street in 1837, and in rooms in Jermyn Street and St James's Street; but it was not until 1862 that he built the house, in accordance with his own

Augustan fancy, on Palace Green, Kensington. Tennyson had been described by Wordsworth in 1845 as "decidedly the first of our living poets," and was on the point of marrying and settling at Twickenham. George Eliot was translating Strauss's *Life of Jesus*. Miss Barrett, of 50 Wimpole Street, had just eloped with the Camberwell-born Robert Browning, who had published *Sordello* and given Miss Barrett's (and Haydon's) close friend, Mary Russell Mitford, material for her later discovery that his work contained "more than I thought." Miss Mitford in this very year still believed that Browning's "acquirements are more remarkable than his poetry."

It will thus be seen that the literary situation had wholly changed. The rationalism of the eighteenth century and the romance of Coleridge, Shelley, and Keats had given place to utilitarianism and determinism. *The Westminster Review* was in existence, employing George Eliot, John Stuart Mill, and other fine free-thinkers. Carlyle was in Cheyne Row; FitzGerald was writing to Frederick Tennyson from Woodbridge that "it is more pleasant to me to sit in a clean room, with a clear air outside and hedges just coming into leaf, rather than in the Tavistock or an upper floor of Charlotte Street"; and the Brontës had published under the pen names of Acton, Currer, and Ellis Bell a small book of their collected poems.

London was still the great centre from which books radiated; authors were born there, and went on living there. But with the irruption and immense popularity of Dickens, and the triumph in 1848 of Macaulay's *History of England*, authorship, especially the authorship of novels, took a remarkable turn. It had ceased in its higher flights to be influenced by the Court, by political or other patrons, by pensions for services rendered or to be rendered, by the tyranny of booksellers, by anything save only popular suffrage. George Eliot and the Brontës might use male pseudonyms; but that was for their own convenience (George Eliot had written an article on *Silly Novels by Lady Novelists*, and obviously could risk no *tu quoque*). Authors no longer trooped to coffee-houses or taverns because their homes were lodgings above oilmen's or ironmongers' shops where food was haphazard. They entertained at houses which they owned or had taken upon lease. Their material circumstances, though they needed still to work hard to maintain them, were immeasurably superior to those of any previous literary generations. The public for new books, in part-form or in volumes, had grown so large that other possibly restrictive influences were for a time overwhelmed.

If such a phenomenon had occurred in our time, it would have been blamed on to the Education Acts of 1870, etc.; but this explanation will not account for a glorious summer of Victorian literacy. Perhaps for once authors and public were in accord. The public wanted to read what the authors wanted to write; and the authors were only a little pecked by those who said that they wrote what the public wanted to read. Today, this would be a self-righteous arraignment; then, it was so trifling that Sydney Smith, writing to tell Dickens how eager some ladies—they happened to be Horace Walpole's Miss Berrys!—were to meet the author of *Nicholas Nickleby* and its successors, assured him that these same ladies would be enchanted to figure as characters in one of his books.

Sydney Smith was very much in the swim; though King George the Third had prophetically said that "he is a very clever man, but he will never be a bishop." He frequented Holland House, the home of a rude and imperious lady who made menials of sages and wits, and who in return, while amusing herself, gave them full opportunity for the enjoyment of each other's conversation. He progressed, when in London, from lodgings in Upper Guilford Street in 1803 to a first entire house, No. 8 Doughty Street; 18 Orchard Street, Portman Square, in 1804; and after becoming Canon of St Paul's, he stayed in Weymouth Street and Stratford Place before buying, first, 33 Charles Street, Berkeley Square, and finally 56 Green Street, Grosvenor Square. He was a socialite; "a mass of fat and muscularity," said Carlyle, "with massive Roman nose, piercing hazel eyes, huge cheeks, shrewdness and fun, seemingly without soul altogether." But he had founded *The Edinburgh Review*, which his friend Jeffrey edited and Hazlitt, Carlyle, and Macaulay wrote for; he once kept the Carlyles laughing for a whole evening; he loved London; and his good heart was so large that it carried him to an accommodation with life never to be reached in Cheyne Row.

Carlyle's weakness was that with a tremendous gift for Old Testament lamentation and denunciation and piercing insight into the defects of all men and all political systems except that of tyranny, he had the simplest and crudest of personal philosophies. His friend Edward FitzGerald said, "Carlyle raves and foams, but has nothing to propose." What Smith proposed was never dithyrambic but always concrete; and he was a great organiser of liberty within the framework of existing society.

Smith and that critical friend, Edward FitzGerald, could have made nothing of the Carlyle household economies. Geraldine Jewsbury said nobody who visited Cheyne Row could tell whether they were poor or rich:

"There were no signs of extravagance, but also," said Froude, " none of poverty. The drawing-room arrangements were exceptionally elegant. The furniture was simple, but solid and handsome; everything was scrupulously clean; everything good of its kind; and there was an air of ease, as of a household living within its means. . . . The rent, which when they came first was 30*l.* a year, I think was never raised—out of respect for Carlyle's character; but it had many rooms in it, which, because they could not bear to have them otherwise, were maintained in the best condition. There was much curiosity among their friends to know how their establishment was supported. Mrs Carlyle had 150*l.* a year from Craigenputtock. He himself, in a late calculation, had set down his average income from his books at another 150*l.*"

It would not have been enough for Smith, Macaulay, or FitzGerald (that "old Fitz" who was named first by Thackeray among those he had loved best in the world); it would not have been enough for Dickens or, once she had tasted means, George Eliot. But it suited Carlyle, who received some American royalties as well as his English earnings; and it enabled him to repulse offers from *The Times* and other periodicals and to remain dyspeptically independent to the end of his life.

FitzGerald's parents were wealthy. They lived in Portland Place, at No. 39. He himself merely lodged, usually in that neighbourhood or in Bloomsbury (7 Southampton Row in 1833, 17 Gloucester Street, Queen Square, in the following year; and frequently, from 1840 to the end of 1848, at No. 19 Charlotte Street or 39 Norton Street, both in the vicinity of Fitzroy Square); but he disliked London, and he removed himself bodily to Suffolk, saying in 1851, "I hate London more and more; but am obliged to be here because of Trusteeships, etc."

With Dickens it was otherwise. True, he fulfilled a childish ambition when in 1856 he bought for £1790 Gadshill Place, on the main road between Rochester and Gravesend. But the poorer streets of London were his true background, because although he was in Chatham between the ages of four and nine, and then saw Gadshill and perhaps unknowingly longed for it, Camden Town was a practical reality, and throughout life his walks took him north, south, east, and west from that centre.

George Augustus Sala, in a well-known description, tells how he often met or saw Dickens "in the oddest places and most inclement weather," from Ratcliffe Highway to Haverstock Hill, Camberwell Green, Gray's Inn Lane, the Wandsworth Road, Norton Folgate, and Kensal New Town.

"A hansom cab whirled you by the Bell and Horns at Brompton, and there he was striding, as with seven-league boots, seemingly in the direction of North-end, Fulham. The Metropolitan Railway sent you forth at Lisson Grove, and you met him plodding speedily towards the Yorkshire Stingo. He was to be met rapidly skirting the grim brick wall of the prison in Coldbath Fields, or trudging along the Seven Sisters-road at Holloway, or bearing, under a steady press of sail, underneath Highgate Archway, or pursuing the even tenor of his way up the Vauxhall-bridge-road."

"In back streets behind Holborn," says Forster; "in Borough courts and passages, in City wharfs or alleys, about the poorer lodging-houses, in prisons, workhouses, ragged-schools, police-courts, rag-shops, chandlers' shops, and all sorts of markets for the poor, he carried his keen observation and untiring study." And besides the houses I have named he was in others, such as that in Chester Place, Regent's Park, while he was waiting for No. 1 Devonshire Terrace to become vacant; 9 Osnaburgh Terrace, Euston Road, for a few weeks in 1844; Tavistock House, in Tavistock Square, where he was from 1851 until he went to Gadshill; 16 Somers Place and 6 Southwick Place, both on the north side of Hyde Park in 1865 and 1866; and 5 Hyde Park Place, opposite the Marble Arch (where now stands a cinema), in 1870. This was his last tenancy in London.

What was he really like? James Bone discovered an old gateman at the Temple who had been an office boy to Dickens, and many times carried his bag to Charing Cross Railway Station for him. This man, when asked for a description, answered, "Well, you wouldn't fancy much the way he was dressed, sir. He had a black velvet coat with big smoked pearl buttons, and trousers of shepherd's plaid, the biggest check you ever saw." George Eliot said he was "not distinguished looking in any way—neither handsome nor ugly, neither fat nor thin, neither tall nor short. . . . His appearance is certainly disappointing—no benevolence in the face, and, I think, little in the head,—the anterior lobe not by any means remarkable." But "what a face is his to meet in a drawing-room!" wrote Leigh Hunt; "it has the life and soul in it of fifty human beings." And Jane Welsh Carlyle, speaking of the eager, restless countenance, said "it was as if made of steel." "A quiet, shrewd looking, little fellow," announced her husband, writing to his brother; "clear blue, intelligent eyes, eyebrows that he arches amaz-ingly, large protrusive rather loose mouth, a face of most extreme *mobility*, which he shuttles about—eyebrows, eyes, mouth and all—in a very singular manner while speaking. Surmount this with a loose coil of common-coloured hair, and set it on a small compact figure, very small, and dressed à la D'Orsay rather than well—this is Pick-wick." Of the readings, Carlyle added, "Dickens does do it capitally, such as *it* is; acts better than any Macready in the world; a whole tragic, comic, heroic *theatre* visible, performing under one hat, and keeping us laughing—in a sorry way, some of us thought—the whole night."

For the rest, Dickens's London is in his books. It is a more vivid London than any other. Did you notice how his London homes moved? At first Camden Town, which is north, but not far north, of Euston Road; Bloomsbury; Euston again; almost back to the bad districts of childhood, where Godwin lived in bleak days; then towards Baker Street, still in a straight line westward from Euston Road; and at last Tyburnia. No farther west than that; never south of the Thames. Perhaps memory of the Marshalsea prison for debtors, where his father, Mr Micawber, spent much time, had an effect. More probably, as, until the 1870s, the Marylebone Road was always "the New Road," the Regent's Park district, being still new and airy, drew him as it was drawing the town.

We know that St John's Wood was a haunt of painters; Landseer went there early and stayed until his death in 1873. Robert Browning, after Mrs Browning's death in Florence in 1861, went to live at 19 Warwick Crescent, Paddington (after 1887 he was at 29 De Vere Gardens); and George Eliot and George Henry Lewes, who had previously lodged at 8 Park Shot, Richmond, and Holly Lodge, Southfields, Wandsworth, rented The Priory, 21 North Bank, Regent's Park, in 1863. This house was to be their home until Lewes's death in 1878; and here they entertained Herbert Spencer, Sir Henry Maine, Jowett, and, on Sundays, increasingly large numbers of serious and admirable Victorian characters. George Eliot's salon, says J. W. Cross, "was important as a meeting-place for many friends whom she cared greatly to see, but it was not otherwise important in her own life—for she was eminently *not* a typical mistress of a *salon*. It was difficult for her, mentally, to move from one person to another. Playing around many disconnected subjects, in talk, neither interested her nor amused her much. She took things too seriously, and seldom found the effort of entertaining compensated by the gain. Fortunately Mr Lewes supplied any qualities lacking in the hostess. A brilliant talker, a delightful *raconteur*, versatile, full of resource in the difficulties of amalgamating diverse groups and bridging over awkward pauses—he managed to secure for these gatherings most of the social success which they obtained."

But both George Eliot and George Henry Lewes were constantly ill or unwell; they were always taking holidays abroad or to Hertfordshire or Surrey in search of air; and at Witley, towards the end of Lewes's life, they found that others, besides themselves, such as the Tennysons, the Du Mauriers, and the Allinghams, preferred the country to London and were making their homes out of town. Ruskin was at Denmark Hill, and Darwin at Down, near Beckenham; the Brontës remained in Yorkshire; and Miss Mitford tended her garden near Reading. Many others lived abroad. If Lewes had not died it seems probable that George Eliot would have abandoned London. After his death, she had no spirit to do so, but married Cross, bought 4 Cheyne Walk, and there died.

The truth is that London was crowding closer and closer about its residents, however far they moved from the centre of it. No longer the oblong of Horace Walpole's account, it had begun to look as it does now upon any detailed map, like an octopus. It did not yet smell of petrol, tar, and rubber. There was no incessant grim rumble from the air as well as from the streets and underground. The bells of telephone and fire engine did not split the ears and nerves of these great people. But stages had given place to omnibuses with inside and outside passengers; and there was so much traffic that one could hear the noise of it from several miles away. The town was getting smokier and more congested; unless, like Godwin and Leigh Hunt, authors were supported by friends, or had come, as Carlyle did, from a poor Scottish home in which toughness and abstinence were bred, those who worked with the brain and the emotions wore out. They died of old age before or soon after sixty; and London knew them no more.

It remained true that, as Hazlitt said, nothing to deserve the name of *society* could be found out of London.

"The very persons that of all others you would wish to associate with in almost any line of life, (or at least of intellectual pursuit,) are to be met there. . . . Individuals may seem lost and hid in the size of the place: but in fact from this very circumstance you are within two or three miles' reach of persons that without it you would be some hundreds apart from. Secondly, London is the only place in which each individual in company is treated according to his value in company, and to that only."

These true words grew more especially obvious with the growth of London. As the middle-aged left it, or died of smoke and exhaustion, there were ever new comers who brought their bright wits and intellects to fresh combat. The old strolling leisure might be gone. Few men thought well to do what Crabb Robinson did, which was to walk from Hampstead by way of Finchley, Colney Hatch, Southgate, Winchmore Hill, and Enfield, to Hornsey and Islington, and back to his lodging in Hatton Garden; all the time reading (although he looked about him, too) Schlegel's *Vorlesungen*. But London was still London; and the best company was to be found there.

Occasionally it came from oversea; and Herman Melville, then the author of *White Jacket*, arrived in 1849 looking for a publisher for that book. He stayed at 25 Craven Street, Strand; took halfpenny steamers at the Adelphi, looked about the Docks, visited the Elephant and Castle, where he extolled the Scotch ale as "the best I ever drunk"; dined in Elm Court, Temple, where he found his hosts as fine a set of fellows as Lamb's Old Benchers; and went to "the beautiful hamlet of Dulwich—the most sequestered, quiet, charming spot indeed." On November 12th, 1849, he

"called on Mr Murray in Albemarle Street. Not in—out of town: took a bus and got out at the Cigar Divan on the Strand. Cheerlessly splendid. Walked to St Paul's, and sat an hour in a dozing state listening to the chanting of the choir. Felt homesick and sentimentally unhappy. Rallied again, and down Ludgate Hill to the London Coffee House to dine with Captain Griswold. . . . Had a noble dinner of turtle soup, pheasant, etc., and glorious wine."

126

Another stranger, but one who was so only as the result of temporary absence in New Zealand, where he was lucky to do well out of sheep, came home in 1864. This was one of the greatest of modern residents; who took rooms at 15 Clifford's Inn, Fleet Street, and occupied them until his death in 1902. The visitor's name was Samuel Butler. He had been born in December 1835, the son and grandson of successful churchmen; and in youth, planning to take Orders in his turn, he had acted as lay assistant to a curate at St James's Church, Piccadilly. When he found that baptised boys were no better than the unbaptised he abandoned the Church and was sent out to New Zealand; where he was so stimulated by loneliness and hatred of his father that a ferment of genius rose in his mind. He returned to London to paint; turned to literature; and lived in Clifford's Inn for nearly forty years in a state of prodigious intellectual activity.

His chambers, said Henry Festing Jones, that big, mild, whispering man who spoke endlessly of Butler with love and—I thought—the least suggestion of malice, and who kept a thousand mementoes of his dead friend at 120 Maida Vale,

"were on the second floor, the north side of the staircase, and consisted of a sitting-room, a bed-room, a painting-room, a pantry, and a passage with cupboards in it. The bed-room and painting-room looked east over Fetter Lane; the sitting-room and pantry looked west over the garden at Clifford's Inn."

Butler needed neither outlook as inspiration; he was absorbed in warfare, always with his father, sometimes with Darwin, sometimes with the Church, sometimes with whatever he did not like. *Wilhelm Meister* was "perhaps the worst book I ever read"; John Morley "I disliked and distrusted"; Morley's *Voltaire* "I disliked very much"; *Aurora Leigh* "I detest it"; Rossetti "I dislike his face and the manner of his work, and I hate his poetry and his friends"; Carlyle was "a wretch"; Bacon was "that old Pecksniff"; *Middlemarch* was "a long piece of studied brag"; "as for the old masters, the better plan would be never to look at one of them, and to consign Raffaelle, along with Socrates, Virgil, Marcus Aurelius Antoninus, Goethe, Beethoven, and another, to limbo, as the Seven Humbugs of Christendom." It would not have mattered where he lived; but it was from Clifford's Inn, looking east over Fetter Lane or west over the garden, that Butler sent a million burning words to a neglectful universe.

To turn from the author of *The Way of All Flesh* to the author of

The Gentle Art of Making Enemies is to turn from a man-eater to a picador; but it is interesting to recall that James McNeill Whistler was born a year earlier than Butler, in 1834. His father was an American soldier and civil engineer who brought the family to Europe (this enabled Whistler to say on one occasion, not quite truthfully, that he had been born in Russia); and James, when fourteen, stayed briefly at 62 Sloane Street with his half-sister, who had married an Englishman. He returned to that unsympathetic address as a young art-student fresh from Paris; and after sharing rooms elsewhere for a time with George du Maurier, he went to what became his famous residence, the White House, in Tite Street, Chelsea, where with superlative audacity he "discovered the night as Turner discovered the sky." In one sense Whistler was the *doyen* of the English-speaking aesthetes; the first of a new order of wits. His gift was not for the savage ridicule of Swift, nor the fine merriment of Sydney Smith; it was for calculated insult, and was based upon a concentrated egotism new, as it seems to me, to our scene. The fop had always been a butt for English writers; now foppishness, armed with derisive genius, was taking the field armed with arrows.

Another dweller in Tite Street, who had more good humour than Whistler, rivalled him in the weapons of wit; but Oscar Wilde was twenty-one years younger, which if he had not taken to evil courses would have given him an overwhelming advantage. He was born in 1854; and Arthur Ransome, writing about him long afterwards, reminded us that in this year

"Leigh Hunt, De Quincey, and Macaulay were alive. Tennyson was writing *Maud* and *The Idylls of the King*. Borrow was wandering in wild Wales and finishing *The Romany Rye*. Browning was preparing *Men and Women* for the press. Dickens was the novelist of the day, and had half a dozen books yet to write. Thackeray was busy on *The Newcomes*. Matthew Arnold was publishing his *Poems*. FitzGerald was working underground in the mine from which he was to extract the roses of Omar. Ruskin had just published *Stones of Venice*, was arranging to buy the work of a young man called Rossetti, helping with the Working Men's College, and writing a pamphlet on the Crystal Palace. William Morris, younger even than Rossetti, was an undergraduate at Oxford, rhyming nightly, and exclaiming that, if this was poetry, it was very easy."

Mr Ransome did not mention that another poet had left Eton in

1853 and, according to Edmund Gosse, entered a region of limbo for two and a half years before arriving at Oxford; but I will name him at this point because Whistler, Swinburne (who was born in 1837), and Butler were contemporaries, and because Whistler and Swinburne were associated in their era as artists and writers with Rossetti, Morris, and George Moore (who was born in 1852). All were in London at the same time; all exercised such fascination over less gifted contemporaries that even today the mention of their names, or of Wilde's name or Aubrey Beardsley's (for so the generations intermingle), stirs the ashes of old controversy.

Rossetti was the eldest of them all, born in 1828. As I have said much earlier in the book, he was born in Charlotte Street, Portland Place; and in youth he was apt to dump himself in the homes of less impecunious friends. He had two celebrated addresses of his own, the first that bleak ménage at 14 Chatham Place, Blackfriars Bridge, where he took his wife, formerly Elizabeth Siddal (or, according to Edmund Gosse, Siddell), and entertained half London until Mrs Rossetti committed suicide; the second, outwardly a plain brick Queen Anne house at 16 Cheyne Walk, Chelsea, but inwardly increasingly dirty, crowded with odd accumulations of china, carving, musical instruments, and Japanese prints and, latterly, with birds and animals and the strangest of human beings.

By contrast, William Morris, as a writer so simple and as a designer so ornate, was respectability personified. His one notable town home was Kelmscott House, the Mall, Hammersmith. Burne-Jones, in 1860, lived in Russell Place, near the British Museum; I have already told how he took Richardson's old dwelling on the North End road; in later life he was out of London altogether. George Moore, returning from Paris, settled in a lodging house in Cecil Street, off the Strand.

"Cecil Street (he wrote in *Confessions of a Young Man*) is remembered with a certain pride, for I went there to live on two pounds a week, determined to make my way in literature . . . . It was in that house in Cecil Street that I began *The Modern Lover*, and wrote it out in copy books from daylight till dark, and then went out to learn London, to assimilate, to become part of the vast incoherent mass which is London. . . . Let me tell you about my rooms. The sitting-room, a good deal longer than it was wide, was panelled with deal, and the deal was painted a light brown; behind it there was a large bedroom, and a big bed stood in the middle of the floor. Next to the

William Morris, from a Caricature by F. Waddy

sitting-room was a small bedroom which was let for ten shillings a week; and the partition wall was so thin that I could hear every movement, and this nearness proved so intolerable that I eventually decided to add ten shillings to my rent and possess myself of the entire flat. In the room above me a pretty young woman lived, an actress at the Savoy Theatre. She had a piano, and she used to play and sing in the mornings, and in the afternoon, friends—girls from the theatre—used to come and see her; and Emma, the maid-of-all-work, used to take them up their tea; and, oh! the chattering and the laughter."

Much later, Moore had what he called a garret in King's Bench Walk; later still, and for the rest of his life, he was at 121 Ebury Street, where he became a sage, talked, dipped his pen in the ink, contemplated the fire and his Aubusson carpet, re-wrote his own stories and certain others of even greater note, and recalled the past with exceptional malice.

It is from his recollection, or what he pretended to recollect, that we learn his personality. He remembered Swinburne, for instance, as a young man, and he recorded the event in an unforgettable anecdote. But before I quote this I must tell you that, like nearly all the great English poets, Swinburne was born in London. The place of his birth was a house in Chester Street, Grosvenor Place. When he was twenty-three, he took rooms at 16 Grafton Street, Fitzroy Square, in order to be within reach of the British Museum. Then he moved in rapid succession to 124 Mount Street, 22A Dover Street, 22 Dorset Street, and 12 North Crescent, Bedford Square, where he spent over four years. In 1877 he had a large sitting-room and a bedroom on the first floor of one of those old flat-faced brick houses of the Bloomsbury age in Great James Street, Bedford Row, so like the Dickens house in Doughty Street or Thackeray's in Coram Street, and so pleasant—as I know from experience—to live in. I once lived at No. 4; E. V. Lucas, I think, had a flat in the same street, and so did Edith Rickert, the American scholar. Swinburne's rooms were at No. 3. Here, amid the ordinary furniture of a lodging house, he arranged his collection of precious glass, his serpentine candlesticks, his mosaic table, and a swinging pier-glass before which, says Gosse, he sometimes performed a ritualistic dance.

George Moore saw Swinburne in this lodging; but not in the sitting-room.

"I remember that one entered the house by an open doorway, as in the Temple, and that I went upstairs, and on the first floor began to wonder on which Swinburne lived; thinking to see a clerk engaged in copying entries into a ledger I opened a door and found myself in a large room in which there was no furniture except a truckle bed. Outside the sheets lay a naked man, a strange, impish little body it was, and about the head, too large for the body, was a great growth of red hair. The fright that this naked man caused me is as vivid in me today as if it had occurred yesterday, possibly more vivid. . . . I just managed to babble out 'Does Mr Jones live here?' The red head shook on a long thin neck like a tulip, and I heard, 'Will you ask downstairs?' I fled."

Two years after this Swinburne was taken by his friend Theodore Watts (afterwards Watts-Dunton) to the semi-detached villa, The Pines, Putney Hill, where he lived for thirty years, and where he died.

A moment ago I said that Oscar Wilde lived in Tite Street. He did so from the time of his marriage in 1884 until the time of his ruin in 1895. On leaving Oxford in 1878 he took some rooms in the Adelphi; and before his marriage he was for a short time in Charles Street, Haymarket. These, as far as I know, were his only addresses in London; and by 1895 the aesthetic movement which had begun with Rossetti and the Pre-Raphaelites and continued with Whistler, Wilde, and the Bodley Head authors and artists had lost momentum. Another realistic period had begun. Novelists, led by Moore, had studied French models; and just as Moore had gone out into the streets "to learn London," so George Gissing and his serious successors sedulously collected material by which things intellectually observed were to be converted into art.

11 *Trollope; Gissing; Henry James; H. G. Wells; Arnold Bennett; Modern authors*

Anthony Trollope was not one of these realists; he did not earnestly walk the London streets, but ambled about the whole country on horseback establishing post-offices, at which, incidentally, his fellow-authors could almost casually post their masterpieces to London publishers. He thus helped to decentralise the profession of letters.

Meredith and Hardy both deserted London; Hardy, once in Trinity Road, Tooting, lived in Dorchester with only trifling visits to the

A. C. Swinburne, from a Caricature by F. Waddy

drawing-rooms of his period; Meredith, after young manhood in London, settled at The Chalet, Box Hill. Trollope himself, having been born in Keppel Street, Russell Square, once passed a summer holiday in his father's chambers in Lincoln's Inn, stayed with his mother in a house at Hadley, near Barnet, and occupied lodgings in Northumberland Street, close to the Marylebone Workhouse. But he was sent by the G.P.O. to Ireland and elsewhere; loved riding to hounds; and, once he had established his independence, made his home at Waltham Cross. If he visited London he stayed at Garland's Hotel in Suffolk Street, Pall Mall.

Of the serious-minded observers of London the most serious was George Gissing, a Yorkshireman of great talent, born in 1857, who wrote long books at immense speed for small rewards on the minimum of nourishment and comfort. Gissing as a youth had been exiled to the United States; but he returned in 1877, and at once began work on the thirty or so novels (at least two of them never published) which he crowded into a quarter of a century of discomfort. He was very poor and often very unhappy. He risked one house after another, from Colville Place and Gower Place, Euston Square, to Islington; by way of Huntley Street, Bedford Square; and other addresses. Even when he found "the most delightful lodgings" on a return visit to Gower Place, he had to move away quickly because the house was insanitary. And so his trek continued, from 29 Dorchester Place, Blandford Square, to 17 Oakley Crescent, Chelsea, which he left because "this house has become very full of people, and the position of my room leaves me scarcely ever in quiet during the evening." On he went, to Milton Street and Rutland Street, Hampstead Road, with a brief unidentified stay in Lambeth in the midst of what proved to be his longest and least unsatisfactory tenancy in London, 7K Cornwall Residences, Marylebone Road. He remained here from 1884 until *Thyrza* was published in 1887 and *The Nether World* had been accepted for serialisation in *The Cornhill Magazine* (no magazine of today would serialise such a book; and James Payn, then editor of *The Cornhill*, deserves honourable memory for his courage); and until Gladstone had gratified him by referring to *The Unclassed* as "speculative and didactic." At the end of September 1888 he left England for the Continent.

His work had been praised by such men as Henry James and two juniors, Arnold Bennett and H. G. Wells, with the latter of whom, towards the end of his life, Gissing became very friendly. Wells, at first enthusiastic, described Gissing finally as a humourless prig; James

Mr and Mrs Carlyle at Home in Cheyne Row, Chelsea: from the painting by Robert Tait in the collection of the Marquis of Northampton

"An Indefatigable Author: or An Idea in the Night."
From a print of 1797

"Homage to Manet": George Moore with his friends at his home in Ebury Street. From the painting by Sir William Orpen, reproduced by kind permission of Manchester City Art Gallery

wrote of his work with respectful reserves; Bennett, according to my memory, showed more than respect in *Fame and Fiction*, but, speaking as a technician, objected that it "offered no cynosure for the eye." James's personal reaction was unfavourable; and an interesting note by Sydney Waterlow which appeared in *The New Statesman* for February 6, 1926, brings both men into focus.

"How surprising" (said Waterlow, speaking of James) "that with so much humming and hawing, such deliberation in the choice of the right adjective, the portraits of persons that he builds up in talk should be so solid and vivid! Thus he described the only occasion on which he had seen Gissing. The impression made by Gissing was a peculiarly painful one. Nature had been unkind to him. The front face was not bad; he had a fine forehead and clustering hair. But when he turned his head you saw one side of the face disfigured by a great expanse of purple scar, and mouth and chin were uncomely and feeble. Altogether an extraordinary, ungainly, common, ill-shaped figure; almost knock-kneed, bearing the unmistakable stamp of Wakefield, his birthplace. And how queer that such a being should speak French so well—with a precise affectation that made it almost too well!"

James's comment shows that, fine and powerful though Gissing could be at his best, he was a misfit. Temperamentally a scholar, he tried to write a *Comédie Humaine* about the inhabitants of a city to which he was always a stranger. He said "the world is for me a collection of phenomena, which are to be studied and reproduced artistically. . . . I watch and observe myself just as much as others." But while watching he did not, I think, penetrate. He was incurably middle-class (what he called "aristocratic") in outlook; and when he said, while visiting Lambeth, that he was "doing my best to get at the meaning of that strange world, so remote from our civilisation," he was confessing a fundamental failure.

Henry James, arriving here from a distance of three thousand miles, was nearer to the "strange world" because by temperament he was a dramatic novelist. He had also a wonderful gift for catching at mystery behind the obvious. He first visited England from New York as a child; and his description of illness in the London hotel in which his family stayed is quite beautiful in colour and emotion.

"I recall in particular certain short sweet times when I could be left alone—with the thick and heavy suggestions of the London room about me, the very smell of which was ancient, strange and impressive, a new revelation altogether, and the window open to the English June and the far-off hum of a thousand possibilities. I consciously took them in, these last, and must then, I think, have first tasted the very greatest pleasure perhaps I was ever to know—that of almost holding my breath in presence of certain aspects to the end of so taking in."

He came again. And as a young man, an artist whose masters were by curious alchemy both Balzac and Turgenev, plus that romantic dream of England created by a reading of Dickens and Thackeray and *Punch*, he came for good. He tried Paris first, only to find that French authors were indifferent to ideas from abroad. But

"that year in Paris was not a lost year—on the contrary. On my way thither I spent something like a fortnight in London; lodging at Story's Hotel, in Dover Street. It was November—dark, foggy, muddy, rainy—and I knew scarcely a creature in the place. . . . And yet the great city seemed to me enchanting.

"You may call it dreary, stupid, dull, inhuman, vulgar," he noted of London. "But I take it as an artist and as a bachelor; as one who has the passion of observation and whose business is the study of human life. It is the biggest aggregation of human life—the most complete compendium of the world."

He walked about the town in a different spirit from that of the realists, "pedestrian gaping having been from childhood prevailingly my line." And for many years, although he travelled a great deal and paid visits to his American home, he was constant to it. He recalls in *The Middle Years* living at 7 Half Moon Street, in "a couple of dusky ground-floor rooms" the walls of which were hung with glazed "coloured" plates from the Christmas numbers of *The Illustrated London News*. From 1879 until certainly 1882, and perhaps longer, he was at 3 Bolton Street, Piccadilly. By 1889, and certainly until 1898, he was at 34 De Vere Gardens, Kensington (Browning was at No 29) : but after 1897 he was a visitor only, for in October of that year he established himself at Lamb House, Rye. It says much for our town that James, however much repelled by some aspects of its inhumanity, lived in and loved it for more than twenty years.

Society—that society which Hazlitt found incomparable—was precious to him. It was similarly precious to H. G. Wells, for a different reason. While James wandered slowly, a stocky, reflective, stout man with protruding eyes, "humming and hawing," but always listening and always absorbing with his own variety of hyperaesthesia the implications of what he saw and heard, Wells plunged among facts and quick interpretations, never at a loss for words, not so much assaying as instantly assessing current values. He was born in Bromley, a district since engulfed in Greater London; and to cockney irreverence he joined an irritable passion for perfectibility which would have been religious if rationalist education had not diverted him to social reform. As a boy he had to touch his hat to the gentry; as a youth he served behind a draper's counter; as a student he had difficulty in supporting himself. By that time he was no longer in the big Sussex house in which his mother was a housekeeper, but in London.

His first lodging here was arranged by his mother. It was in a crowded, "extensively sub-let" little house in Westbourne Park; and after scuffling with his landlady Wells moved on to a "gaunt house" at 181 Euston Road, the home of his father's sister-in-law. Here he met his cousin and first wife. Events took him away from town; it was not until 1888 that he was back in a room in Theobald's Road, which he rented for four shillings a week.

"It was not really a room but a partitioned-off part of an attic; it had no fireplace, and it was furnished simply with a truckle bed, a wash-hand-stand, a chair and a small chest of drawers carrying a looking-glass. The partition was so thin, that audibly I was, so to speak, in the next room. My neighbours were a young couple on whom I never set eyes, but their voices became very familiar to me and I learnt much about their intimate lives. When the intimacy seemed to be rising to a regrettable level, I would cough vigorously, make my bed creak or move my chair about, and the young couple would instantly sink out of existence into a profound silence like a frightened fish in a deep pool."

Then he re-discovered his aunt, who had abandoned "the gaunt house in Euston Road" and was acting as housekeeper in Fitzroy Road, near Regent's Park. In no time he had gone to live in her care; and by 1891 he took a small house at 28 Haldon Road, East Putney, and married his cousin. This house was changed for one at 4 Cumnor Place, Sutton; but the marriage came to an abrupt end about Christmas-time, 1893, so that, forsaking Sutton, Wells found himself back in London. He was in lodgings, first at 7 Mornington Place and then at 12 Mornington Road, both in the neighbourhood of Camden

Town. 1896 saw him at Lynton, Maybury Road, Woking, Surrey, outside the London area; at the end of that year he was at Heatherlea, Worcester Park; and in 1897 he abandoned London for Sandgate.

When I first met Wells, in 1912, after I had published a book on Gissing which he liked, he was in that delightful old-fashioned country road in the heart of Hampstead called Church Row. My recollection is that the drawing-room, on the first floor, went from the front to the back of the house; and that by daylight one saw from the back window a most agreeable garden in which two small boys fought each other with wooden swords. At night one did not so much dance as prance to the music of a treadle-pianola, led by the host. That would be characteristic. I do not know what the neighbours thought of the noise. In any case it did not matter; because shortly afterwards Wells entered into occupation of Little Easton Rectory (re-named Easton Glebe), near Dunmow; and his London address was a flat at St James's Court, Buckingham Gate.

Then, for several years, he was at 4 Whitehall Court (Bernard Shaw went to Whitehall Court after leaving Adelphi Terrace; and Lady Russell, the author of *Vera* and *Elizabeth and Her German Garden*, also had a flat there); and after Mrs Wells's death, until he moved to his final home, a house at 13 Hanover Terrace, Regent's Park, he was for some months at Chiltern Court, over Baker Street Station, exactly two floors above the palatial, corridored establishment of Arnold Bennett.

It was necessary to Wells to have the stimulation of company; and he was always at his best at home. There he talked with a living sense of mischief, and there, although impetuous and easily moved to irritability, he brimmed with affectionate improvisations. The blue eyes roamed; he piquantly narrated stories in which grave men's vanities became farcical; and he listened to the ideas of other men and transfigured them. You saw his head nod emphatically; he busily captured and synthesised whatever was valuable to him; and the result was that extraordinary output of rapid writing, so fluent, so invariably happy in epithet, in which past and future were given life, bias, and mortality. Wells joined a number of clubs. I should not have said he was a good clubman. He liked to be at home; and his homes had an unceremonious ease natural to the man.

Arnold Bennett's homes were less unceremonious. He was an exact man, who sat upright and gave so much thought to his surroundings that if he had had less humour he would have seemed house-proud. He came to London from the Potteries when he was twenty-one; and the only addresses of his youth which are known to me are (in 1890) 46 Alexandra Road, Hornsey, and (ten years later) 9 Fulham Park Gardens. My impression is that he portrayed the latter house in *The Roll-Call*. But once he had resigned the editorship of *Woman* he went to live in Berkshire; and once he had lived in Berkshire he went, in emulation of George Moore, to Paris.

Returning to England in 1911, he presently set up house—a house centrally-heated, newly-painted, and full of Empire furniture—at Thorpe-le-Soken, in Essex, near enough to the yachting ports to allow him the pride and solitude of his barge-built *Velsa*. He then had no London address; but on his visits stayed at different hotels. When the first World War began, however, it was necessary for him, in connection with his work for the Press and the Ministry of Information, to have a *pied à terre* in town. He made an arrangement by which he furnished for himself and occupied as a flat two communicating rooms at the top of the Royal Thames Yacht Club at 80 Piccadilly. In these rooms he hung modern paintings; the chairs were comfortable; the upholstery a beautiful blue; and the place was a most agreeable resort. Bennett was complacent and content.

These, however, were bachelor quarters; and after the war he and Mrs Bennett had a large handsome flat on the first and upper floors of a house called 12B George Street, Hanover Square. They remained there until they separated in 1921. When Bennett moved alone to 75 Cadogan Square he gave up the Thorpe-le-Soken house and achieved new splendours. His pictures were again modern; his drawing-room glittered and was comfortless; but the dining-room, entirely Victorian, was irresistible. When I first visited this house I objected brusquely to the whim of some previous occupant, who had panelled every door with mirrors. I said, "I couldn't stand all this looking-glass!" Bennett, the least vain of men, replied blandly: "I . . . was born for it."

In November 1930 he went to 97 Chiltern Court, Clarence Gate, to a pair of sumptuous flats which had been converted into one; and it was soon after arriving here and installing steel bookshelves and many modernities especially gratifying to his temper that he visited France, caught typhoid fever, and became fatally ill. I shall never forget the sight of that corner of Marylebone Road and Upper Baker Street early in 1931. The roadway was deep in straw; a phenomenon I had not seen for many years, and never in such a thoroughfare.

Of Bennett's contemporaries few were true London residents. Joseph Conrad was at all times in the country. John Galsworthy had a house, a fine big house with fine big iron gates, at North Row, Hampstead; but his real home was at Bury, overlooking the Sussex Downs, or at Manaton, in Devonshire. Rudyard Kipling, flirting with London at the age of twenty-four, "short, sturdy, bullet-headed, with very sharp eyes behind his defensive glasses," spent several months in Villiers Street in 1900 and was told by Edmund Gosse to "go back to the Far East." A. E. W. Mason, when not roving the world, lived in South Street, Mayfair. Somerset Maugham, after studying life at St Thomas's Hospital, as he pictures it in *Of Human Bondage* and *Liza of Lambeth*, preferred foreign parts. Edward Garnett, the publishers' reader who discovered Conrad and Galsworthy, was in Chelsea—on the second floor of 19 Pond Place. Gilbert Chesterton was in Prince of Wales Mansions, Battersea Park; and his neighbour, Philip Gibbs, who wrote an apposite novel entitled *Intellectual Mansions, S.W.*, has told me that Chesterton, even then suffering from serious heart trouble, climbed the stairs very slowly indeed and kept a growler waiting for his journeys to Fleet Street.

It would obviously be impossible for me to summon all the London homes of these and other modern writers without challenging the Post Office Directory. You may think I have already gone far enough in that direction. But since I have referred to several of my immediate contemporaries in the chapter on publishers, I will conclude by saying that in 1919 I was encouraged by my mother to leave her and live by myself in the heart of London. By the kindness of two persons I was enabled to do this; for Mrs Desmond MacCarthy, determined to get the help of Roger Fry in a search for rooms, met Bertrand Russell on her way to Fry's home and secured me a generous landlord for the next five years. During those years I lived in a studio in Fitzroy Street and a flat in Russell Chambers, Bury Street, Bloomsbury.

I thus became a man about town. I was already acquainted with several authors; but the number of them was largely increased. In those days Bertrand Russell himself lived at 31 Sydney Street, Chelsea; Walter de la Mare at 14 Thornsett Road, Anerley, close to the Crystal Palace; Hugh Walpole was in chambers in Ryder Street, St James's. Walpole was later in a first-floor flat at 90 Piccadilly, on the north side, overlooking the Green Park. St John Ervine and his wife were at Golders Green; Gilbert Cannan had a studio in Elm Tree Road, St John's Wood; J. D. Beresford had left a charming but remote country dwelling at Winslow, in Buckinghamshire, to act as literary adviser for Messrs Collins and to live in Notting Hill. Driving one night to dinner with him, I was forced to leave a small unlockable car outside the house. I said to the maid: "Is this an honest neighbourhood?" She answered "not very." But the car was still there when I left the house, and no doubt she slandered Notting Hill.

Compton Mackenzie, whom I met in Martin Secker's office, was then at The Cottage, North Street, Westminster. "The tall narrow house in Kensington" of the early pages of *Sinister Street* was in Avonmore Road. Mackenzie's parents moved from this address to Nevern Square; and his own married life began in Grosvenor Road, on the Embankment. The Cottage, North Street, consisted of two old cottages knocked into one (this is now demolished), situated behind the houses on the south side of the street. Access to it was by way of a narrow covered passage, with a hall-door between two of the houses. I think the number was six. Hilaire Belloc and Maurice Baring had both formerly occupied the cottage. But Mackenzie's health called for a warmer climate than the English; and after his military service in the First World War he was much out of England. Only for a short time did he later, like Leigh Hunt, experiment with the seven airs of Hampstead, where he had a house in the Vale of Health. Maurice Baring had moved to Dulwich Village; Hilaire Belloc to Horsham; Chesterton to Beaconsfield; Shaw to Ayot St Lawrence. London was ready for new generations.

I have tried to show you where the authors of two and a half centuries lived in town; how they lived in the city when only the wealthy were outside its walls; that when theatre and pulpit were of less moment than the Court and the Court's political favourites, they moved to St. James's; that when statesmen ceased to be patrons they turned to Fleet Street and Paternoster Row; that when the public began to be widely interested they could afford to follow their own whims; and that while Chelsea held its own, as it does today, during Queen Victoria's reign, Hampstead, St John's Wood, and Regent's Park became increasingly popular until ease of transport enabled a man to live wherever he liked.

Since 1914 we have seen Bloomsbury revive, first as the home of intellect, and now as the home of publishers. St John's Wood is an even newer fashion for intellect. But many leading authors do not see London from one month's end to another. Whether they are wise to absent themselves I do not attempt to say. In the next chapter I shall show what they may miss through failure to muster with the rest in the major haunts of literary society.

VI

The Haunts Of Writers

1 *The British Museum; Marian Edwardes; The London Library; the National Central Library; Dr. Williams's Library*

I suppose the most famous London haunt of literary men and women to be the British Museum Reading Room. There, under that enormous dome, at desks radiating from its centre like the spokes of a wheel, sit, hour after hour and month after month, students, scholars, hacks, bibliographers—all to whom continuous reading is a necessity of life. And the setting is worthy of their task. There is a height in this great room, a cathedral-like silence in which a cough or a dropped book echoes and becomes a crime, a monumental air of dignity and opulence in the supply of books, that I have always felt to be inspiring. Not inspiring as natural beauty is inspiring; but scholastically exemplary. One says to oneself: "I *will* learn; I *will* master what I have come here to master." Many must have mastered what they came to master. Not I.

There is a scent of warmth. There are the almost noiseless librarians who slide books on to the desk at one's side. There is that great assembly of catalogues which one draws out by leather loops. And there are the people seated, many of them sprawling, at the desks. They, indeed, are wonderful. Some are precise; they have come for immediate purpose, and they remain only until they have found what they need. Others browse. There are old men who cast aside red mufflers but do not cast aside greatly-worn overcoats; there are those of all ages, seeking "authorities" and material for busy monographs, gratifying the daily needs of editors and publishers, who desire innumerable facts about old books or authors. I have read, even, that there was formerly— although I never saw him—an old, white-bearded negro in a bowler hat who was every day in the same seat, and whose incalculable studies ended only with his mysterious disappearance. Did he die, evaporate, learn everything? Nobody can tell. Lenin is said to have sat there; Swinburne lodged near the Museum so that he might attend daily; at different times I have met half the literary men of my own era, absorbed and—for a while—happy.

When I was at Dents we employed a devoted and selfless woman,

Miss Marian Edwardes. She made indexes; she sought the detail for many introductions and bibliographies for Everyman's Library. She was short, untidy, grizzle-haired, rather bustling, with a loud high voice; and she always carried a big bag, I suppose of leather, which was crammed with scraps of paper bearing the results of endless ill-paid research. But she was not only a publishers' tracker. Month after month, quietly and assiduously, she was gathering material for a *magnum opus*. What was it, you ask? I had forgotten. I have just found the title. It was *A Summary of the Literature of Modern Europe (England, France, Germany, Italy, Spain) to A.D. 1400*. Does not the very name of that book cause a fainting of the spirit? It caused Miss Edwardes no faintness; it was her *Divine Comedy*, her *Hamlet*, her *War and Peace*. She was a good and brave woman. And she was accurate.

One of the lessons I learned at Dents was the art of revision or inter-polation. I saw what Miss Edwardes brought in, and what Ernest Rhys made of it. He took two or three exercise-book pages of her scratchy writing, changed the order of words, inserted other words, and deleted all that were superfluous. Dead phrases came alive; they had been worked on by poetic intelligence. This was Rhys's speciality. He was a journalist and hack editor; but he gave quality to everything he did, and when he visited the Reading Room in the course of his work it became a club and a mint. When I was at Dents I thought him a strange, silent, unfriendly man (Miss Edwardes said "So different from Mr Macdonald," the editor of Lamb, and her favourite); but when I met him after leaving Dents I realised that he was only reserved in the manner of one who dwelt much alone. He told bitter stories of Dent with agreeable tartness.

We owe this Reading Room, of which the present building arose long after his day, to a Scots-Irish naturalist and physician, Sir Hans Sloane. In a life-time of more than ninety years Sloane collected fifty thousand books and over three thousand five hundred manuscripts; and after his death in 1753 they were offered to the nation. Twenty thousand pounds having been raised by a lottery, the collections were assembled—with others—in Montagu House. They were in charge of one Principal Keeper, three Librarians, and three Assistants; and, as scientific works preponderated, the Keeper and two senior Librarians were all Doctors of Medicine.

This was in and immediately after 1756, for the Reading Room as we know it is not yet a hundred years old; and what poor scholars in London did before civilisation was achieved, I do not know. Johnson is said in Boswell's *Life* to have read at the Queen's House.[1] Gibbon, as late as 1779, wrote that "the greatest city in the world is still destitute of a public library; and the writer who has undertaken to treat any large historical subject is reduced to the necessity of purchasing, for his private use, a numerous and valuable collection of books." Even Carlyle, when he was writing *The French Revolution*, had to forgo the use of important French pamphlets, known to be in the Museum, because they were "inaccessible"; for later work he was fed, through kind scholar friends, from the University Library at Cambridge.

It was this last obligation, because a writer on any historical subject needs his authorities ever at hand, that made Carlyle dream of a grand lending library for the service of professionals; and the London Library is the result of that dream. "He set on foot," Froude says, "an agitation," which was supported by men of influence; and the agitation was triumphant. The year was 1839. There in the far north-western corner of St James's Square lies our servant; within it stands a bust of Carlyle and a big, ornate clock once belonging to John Forster; and behind these symbolic pieces every kind of help in work and relaxation, from bound volumes of old periodicals to the newest biography or even the newest novel. What an incomparable boon!

The pleasure the London Library gives has always been heightened for me by its staff, whose names, with two exceptions, I have never learned. But I rejoice in one who was in the Library when I first visited it fifty years ago, and who is still there. Mr Cox as a boy saw Carlyle; for seventy years he has observed all the authors who have used the library; his recollections, brief, occasional, and unstudied are vivid portraits for the curious. That he has read every book in the London Library is impossible; that he knows all that every book contains seems unquestionable. He is a character and a miracle.

Clubs such as the Reform and Athenaeum have fine collections; and the chief Public Libraries are excellent. Two other libraries should be mentioned as being of particular help to students. The first is the National Central Library in Malet Place, off Great Russell Street, which is in effect a great book exchange, enabling libraries throughout England to borrow from each other for the service of poor readers. The second is Dr Williams's Library, at 16 Grafton Street, between Tottenham Court Road and Gower Street. This was founded

[1] Buckingham House, bought by George III in 1761 and settled on Queen Charlotte. Buckingham Palace now occupies the site.

in 1724 with money bequeathed by the Rev. Daniel Williams. Its most celebrated possession, for book-lovers, consists of the original manuscripts of Crabb Robinson's *Diary and Reminiscences*. Only portions of this immensity of documents have been published. The whole mass covers personal memoirs of every leading English and German writer of several generations, from Goethe to Thackeray and F. W. Newman. It begins in 1781 and ends in 1867; and it is the result of such fluent acquaintance that Walter Bagehot, fearing an old man's copiousness and indiscretion, confessed to panic at hearing that it was to be made public. However, Bagehot found little amiss; and as for ourselves, who know how indiscreet modern writers are as a matter of pride, we feel only delight at possessing a ruby among auto-biographies.

2 *Coffee-houses; Taverns; Restaurants*

So far I have spoken of libraries. You may ask whether the sole concern of authors is with books. It is not. If I feel that bookish authors enjoy too great a critical prestige compared with those who create, this, no doubt, is because, like Jane Austen, I reject the notion that novel-writing is an inferior art. I think it as difficult to be a scholar in human nature as to be a scholar in a dead language. On the other hand I like and admire many of the scholars I have met, because, like novelists, they are simple creatures. If they seem aloof, the reason is that they are shy; and novelists, of course, cannot be shy. If they were shy they would learn nothing whatever about the human beings who are their raw material.

In hunting for knowledge of life, and for heroes to publish their earliest works, young novelists or potential novelists grow gregarious, and meet at literary circles, at public houses, studios, tea parties, supper parties, restaurants, and clubs. At literary circles, of which there are many in London, they listen to lectures, or to papers read by other rising stars; they take part in discussions; they go away from brave occasions feeling that fame—is it only fame?—is just round the corner. If they have been to public school and university they may have learnt to take either side in argument with equal skill. If they have not enjoyed such training they rely on consciousness of talent. But they must talk; it is an exaltation similar to that of young animals romping; and is natural to fresh, eager wits.

It has ever been so. Beaumont's lines about the Mermaid Tavern, addressed to Ben Jonson, are almost over-familiar:

> What things have we seen
> Done at the Mermaid! Heard words that have been
> So nimble, and so full of subtle flame,
> As if that every one from whence they came
> Had meant to put his whole wit in a jest,
> And had resolv'd to live a fool the rest
> Of his dull life.

Jonson was also a king in the West Apollo Room of the Devil Tavern, by Temple Bar, "a place sacred to Mirth, tempered with Discretion, where Ben Jonson and his Sons used to make their Liberal Meetings" and where "the Rules of Ben's Club are in Gold Letters over the Chimney."

We know, too, that Will's Coffee-house, which was above the premises of a woollen-draper in Bow Street, had what was known as the wits' room on the first floor, where Dryden went every evening to talk as a master among lesser men, and where aspirants to letters listened, crept closer, and sometimes dared their way into the conversation. We know that *The Tatler*, promising in April 1709, to date all its accounts of poetry from Will's, and of learning from the Grecian Coffee-house, remarked that it could not keep an ingenious man to go daily to Will's under twopence a day for his expenses, nor to the Grecian without allowing him some of the plain Spanish snuff, fashionable since 1702, so that he might be "as able as others at the learned table." We therefore have the sense of being brought close to greatness, almost to Dryden's chair.

That sense is unjustified. Nothing is known of Dryden's manner, save only that a single anecdote is recorded of him by a man who ventured once to contradict, and found his contradiction well-received. Dryden had no Boswell; his prime had passed before the literary wits were in full flourish; he was "not a very genteel man." So he remains a legend, the hero of Will's Coffee-house, a great poet and critic and a lesser dramatist; but otherwise as remote as Shakespeare.

With the death of Dryden, Will's grew less important; it was quite eclipsed when Addison took his friends Steele, Budgell, Ambrose Philips, Carey, and Davenant over the way to Button's, which was in Russell Street, two doors from Covent Garden. Addison used to breakfast with one or other of these men at his lodgings in St James's Place, dine and sup at taverns, and spent the evening in talk at Button's. He made the house. When he died, and Steele left London, and the wits were dispersed, it and other such coffee-houses yielded to successors. Dr Johnson still went on special occasions to the Devil Tavern; but his dearer loves were Joe's, in Mitre Court, Fleet Street; the Turk's Head, in Gerrard Street, where "the Club" (founded by himself and Reynolds) met; and the Essex Head, in Essex Street, Strand, where he formed a small club in order to patronise the landlord, an old servant of the Thrales. Never to the Cheshire Cheese.

He called them clubs; they were small gatherings of men for talk, and except that coffee-houses kept late hours they were not unlike the gatherings one may still see at the end of the day in city tea-shops or taverns in Bloomsbury or Soho or Chelsea. The talk was perhaps better; it was more leisurely and had more to do with literature; but not all the talkers were worth reporting, and coffee-house gatherings demanded that one man, a Great Cham, venerated for his gifts, should lead the discourse.

Gibbon speaks of the Cocoa-tree, at 64 St James's Street, where "twenty or thirty, perhaps, of the first men in the kingdom in point of fortune or fashion" would sup "at little tables covered with a napkin, in the middle of a coffee-room, upon a bit of cold meat, or a sandwich, and drinking a glass of punch." But this was an assembly of Bute's supporters; it had no connection with books. The Chapter-house in Paul's Alley, Paternoster Row, came closer to them. In fact it came very close indeed, not only in the eighteenth century but later; for the Brontë sisters stayed there—"a strange place, but they did not well know where else to go"—on their first visit to London in 1848; and Mr Town, writing in the first number of *The Connoisseur* on January 31st, 1754, before mentioning the Bedford, in Covent Garden, "where almost everyone you meet is a polite scholar and a wit," visited St Paul's, and wrote that

"my publisher would not forgive me, was I to leave the neighbourhood without taking notice of the Chapter coffee-house, which is frequented by those encouragers of literature, and (as they are stiled by an eminent critic) 'not the worst judges of merit,' the booksellers. The conversation here naturally turns upon the newest publications; but their criticisms are somewhat singular. When they say a *good* book, they do not mean to praise the stile or sentiment, but the quick and extensive sale of it. That book in the phrase of the

147

CONGER is best, which sells most: and if the demand for *Quarles* should be greater than for *Pope*, he would have the highest place on the rubric-post."

The Conger has its modern successors; the Publishers' Circle, the Double Crown Club, the Paternoster Club, and others. The Paternosters mingle authors with members of the trade; the others are more concerned with problems of the trade's parlous condition. Modern publishers, also, take broader views than the Conger did of quality in literature. The Paternoster (meeting for lunch), like the Society of Bookmen (which meets for dinner), is not primarily a conversation club, as Johnson's were; and neither compares with the coffee-house gatherings of Dryden's or Addison's day. There is a speaker; there are supplementary speeches, guests, hospitality, and much good-fellowship; but there is no Great Cham and the members would feel self-conscious if they were called on to emulate Jonson, Johnson, or Addison. Few of today's wits, once they have become great, wander abroad to coffee-houses or taverns. Even if they go, their visits are short. Appointments call them elsewhere.

This does not apply to the younger men, of course. There are several taverns, and a few restaurants, where such men gather; where they talk at large; and where, it may be, some of the ancient spirit revives. During the Second World War, the most familiar of these taverns was the Wheatsheaf, in Rathbone Place. This is still in existence; but artists, art students, young poets, and yet younger reviewers tend nowadays to visit another tavern, farther along Rathbone Place, the Black Horse, which they do in considerable numbers on Saturday nights. Or they may go to the Old Queen's Head across the street at the corner of Soho Street and Oxford Street, and the Fitzroy, in Charlotte Street.

In Soho proper, the York Minster (or the French Pub) has a considerable literary and artistic clientèle, some of whom lunch or assemble early in the evening; and in old Bloomsbury the Lamb in Lamb's Conduit Street, or the Museum Tavern, opposite the British Museum, have regular patrons. In the neighbourhood of Broadcasting House the favourites are the Stag's Head in New Cavendish Street; the George, in Great Portland Street; and Pagani's. In Chelsea are the Nelson, in King's Road; the Eight Bells, on the Embankment; and the Crosskeys, in Lawrence Street. All these are very different from Will's, or Button's, or The Turk's Head; but so are the frequenters.

The one similarity they have is that they go to these places in order to be with men of their own stamp, just as the coffee-house men did. It may be that what they say is quite as memorable as the un-recorded wisdom of Dryden.

Restaurants are used less for gatherings of men for talk than for quiet interchange between two, or at most four, persons. I do not think any one of the modern restaurants has the character of the old Café Royal, even as it was during and after the First World War, but cer-tainly as it was in the gas-lit nineties. It was easy to persuade yourself in 1920, amid the still-existing red plush seats of the brasserie, that you were in Paris; almost as easy to imagine the presence at other tables of Wilde, Rothenstein, Max Beerbohm, and the rest of that extraordinary clientèle. I cannot speak as confidently of later years, although James Agate used to go to the Café Royal to the end of his life; and no doubt had his circle.

In the years 1918–23 I often lunched at the Monico, in Piccadilly Circus, almost always with Martin Secker, but also with Gilbert Can-nan, Compton Mackenzie, Francis Brett Young, and others of the generation grouped about Secker. Viola and Francis Meynell came occasionally. It now seems extraordinary that we should have relished a place which had a band; but we were merry there, and I think the talk was good. I never hear the song, *Roses in Picardy*, which was then in vogue, without re-entering that great room in spirit and re-living old sensations.

Oddenino's was another restaurant popular with writers; and there was a succession of interesting small places in Soho, from Kettner's to the Moulin d'Or. Morley Roberts, Gissing's friend, penitent at having felt unable to be helpful about Gissing, took me to the Rendez-vous in 1912; in 1918, I think, Arnold Bennett, who heard quickly of any place where there was good cooking, introduced me to the Commercio, in Frith Street; Hugh Walpole and I generally went to the Isola Bella, on the east side of the Street. It was Bennett who took me first to a very small, unknown restaurant in West Street, Charing Cross Road, called the Ivy. That was during the First World War and our companion at the feast was E. A. Rickards, the architect. The Ivy has since become an institution; and most literary and theatrical people have gone there for the last thirty years. Some now favour the Caprice, in Arlington Street, where the Ivy's old maître d'hôtel, Mario, is manager, and where the old Ivy atmosphere survives. Both these restaurants have kept a high quality in hard times; in both, habitués feel themselves surrounded by something more than politeness; and they are usually full of familiar faces.

Another place, noted in its day and until the early thirties, was the great Restaurant de la Tour Eiffel, kept by Stulik, an Austrian, in the house now occupied by The White Tower in Percy Street, Tottenham Court Road. "Discovered" by Augustus John or Madame Strindberg (perhaps by both), and always unconcerned with any form of austerity, it was famous all over Europe, so that distinguished writers and artists from every quarter met and fraternised at its tables. Chief among these was John; lesser men came and went as circumstances allowed; the company was always fine and cosmopolitan.

I have not mentioned Rule's, in Maiden Lane, where writers go; and I must do so. This is a good, quiet, unpretentious place. Other restaurants patronised by writers are Pitt's, in Old Compton Street, and the Akropolis, in Percy Street. Many Bloomsbury-housed publishers use the Étoile, in Charlotte Street. And of course I must speak of the Savoy Grill, where some of the richest gatherings I ever experienced were held.

The host on these occasions was George Doran, the American publisher, an Irish-Canadian who loved London and London authors, and who with superb gallantry brought them together, regardless of expense. I always felt that Doran, with his fine figure and presence, would have made a grand ambassador; and he loved entertaining. He gave four types of dinner; the first for oneself alone. That meant business. The second was an omnium gatherum of talent, male and female. I was never invited to one of these. The third was for a dozen or twenty men; peers, ambassadors, M.P.s, scholars, and artists might join the authors. The fourth, a very rare treat, was one for which the guests were what he called hand-picked. One such party included H. G. Wells, Max Beerbohm, Somerset Maugham, A. P. Herbert, Philip Gibbs, Arnold Bennett, John Drinkwater, and C. B. Cochran; and I still recall snatches of conversation from that party which I must not now repeat because some of those present are still alive. On the whole this was as good an instance as I could give of men talking well for the pleasure it would give to others whom they liked. I would match the interchange against anything heard at Button's.

3 The Clubs

Finally, there are the Clubs—not clubs in Johnson's sense; but solid institutions developed from the political and gambling clubs of the

Victorian Fleet Street

The British Museum Reading Room

Charing Cross Road

eighteenth century, where at Brooks's men like Fox lost fortunes in a
night and men like Lord Ossory or Lord Bolingbroke won them by
betting on trifles.

Such post-gambling clubs enjoyed their great day in times past,
when Thackeray and Dickens could meet and quarrel over the question
whether Edmund Yates should or should not be expelled from the
Garrick because he had written impudently of Thackeray in *The
World*, and when old men sat hour after hour in the best chairs dis-
cussing the classics or imagining the doom of the British Empire. I
have heard tell of such days; one very old friend used to make our
mouths water by remembering how men lunched for eightpence,
with beer and cheese thrown in, and drank champagne for dinner with
saddle of mutton and suchlike viands as a prelude to port and the
best of intellectual stimulant.

Even I remember that in comparative youth I spent evenings in
good company casually gathered by the accident of arrival. In 1951
the Club is an anachronism. It belongs to an era when men could afford
to be self-indulgent, when by saying "I am going to the Club" they
could be assured of immunity from the company of females. They no
longer indulge themselves; they enjoy no immunities. And they have
no time. Only here and there in London do amateurs discuss great
literature over port or coffee; and most such amateurs are rarely-
endowed bachelors or widowers. In fact

> The world is too much with us; late and soon,
> Getting and spending, we lay waste our powers:
> Little we see in Nature that is ours.

By half past two in the day, smoking-rooms are empty but for solitaries
needing an afternoon nap; at night dining-rooms echo only with
whispers from waiters who ask whether members will quaff beer, water
or cyder, and many tables are empty; by ten o'clock the places are
deserted. At all times they are full of ghosts; the ghosts of dead friends
and recollected laughters.

Let us not fall, however, into the melancholy of old age. I am a great
believer in counting one's blessings; perhaps because I have personally
a great many to count. And I think we should bear in mind that
authors now have a club of their own, with a club-house at 62 and 63
Glebe Place, Chelsea. This is the P.E.N., an international fraternity of
all writers and editors whose Governments allow them to know each
other. I am not myself a frequenter of the P.E.N. club-house (although

I am a member of the P.E.N.), because, to tell the truth, I cannot bear writers en masse; but the P.E.N.'s work for international understanding and cooperation is a beam of light in a vituperative world.

The clubs where the small groups I prefer used to gather, and still infrequently gather, offer a more general background than the P.E.N. They embrace painters (always good talkers and well-read men), barristers (with the most fascinating "shop" in the world), doctors, and learned Civil Servants. Perhaps they should be called civil savants? I remember with delight, in this connection, the dinner-parties given by E. V. Lucas at the old Orleans Club, in King Street, St. James's, at which one met even publishers; while the host, fundamentally an unhappy man, forgot his disappointments in the pleasure of seeing scholars hobnob with novelists, dramatic critics with court officials, and witnessing the uniform mystification of these cultured men by the best conjuror I ever hope to see. The parties varied; host and conjuror were constant.

At the Press Club the company consists for the most part of active journalists, artists, and those connected in some business capacity with daily or weekly journals. The club, hidden away behind Fleet Street, in Salisbury Square, is well situated for these men; and it is a home of legend. I do not mean that it is a place where fairy tales are told; no, but it is haunted by memory of certain men, journalists of old fame, such as Charlie Hands and Edgar Wallace. Hands is the subject of innumerable tales; you may see him in pen-and-ink originals of which so many hang on the walls of the club, and hear of his exploits whenever you meet a journalist. A small man with his hands in his pockets and a pointed nose and the smile of Robin Goodfellow; whose resource was never found wanting. "Charlie . . ." begins somebody. All begin to beam. Not less noteworthy was Edgar Wallace, a legend in himself; a man whose stories went all over the world, with never one salacious or suggestive episode in them. He was proud of this fact; would talk quietly and unboastfully, white, impassive, without gesture, always as it were in an undertone, smoking his cigarettes and keeping as sober as the Sphinx. He gave no impression of haste; he moved through the Press Club, as he moved everywhere, with recognitions and always uncynical, unimpressible kindness. These are not the only legendary figures of the club; the place is full of such figures. Both are outstanding.

I do not suppose the Authors' Club, in Whitehall Court, to be as full of legend; but it must have many stories to tell. For me it is memorable because when I was twenty-five Arnold Bennett, newly returned from France, invited me to lunch with him there. He was at the height of his first fame, having followed the success of *The Old Wives' Tale* with *Clayhanger*; and he showed me that day the unfinished manuscript of *Hilda Lessways*. Bennett was rather stiff; I was conscious of my youth. But as we sat at the luncheon table he remarked: "Over there . . . is the best-selling novelist in . . . Great Britain." I said in marvel: "Not *Charles Garvice*!" It was Charles Garvice.

In this year of 1951, Charles Garvice is probably forgotten; but in 1911 he had with less sophisticated readers such a vogue as can hardly be exaggerated. He had in younger days written large numbers of serial stories for a popular journal, selling them outright to the proprietors; then, having caught the public taste, he made so much money that he was able to buy the periodical entire, and thus repossess himself of his own copyrights. Success continued; he had an inexhaustible supply of books to publish; and he lunched, I believe, every day at the Authors' Club. Bennett said: "He . . . is a . . . very decent chap."

I told you how, when I was at Dents, we could hear revelry above, coming from the Yorick Club. I can now admit that I never went to that club; for it had ceased to exist by the time I began to visit clubs. The only member I knew was Walter Jerrold, a small man who looked like an old actor, and who wore a monocle with a broad black ribbon. He was the grandson of Douglas Jerrold, the famous Victorian novelist and journalist; and was the first I ever heard to pronounce Charles Lamb's pen-name as I believe it should be pronounced, "Ellia." He called in at Dents on his way to the Yorick, which, to judge by the noise we heard, must have been convivial. That is all I know about the club or its membership.

Another convivial club, the Savage, used to be in Adelphi Terrace; and I always regret that it had to move from there. I was often taken into it by St John Adcock, one of the best of modern Londoners. He was an old journalist, a writer about books and men, full of anecdote, and, round about 1910, editor of *The Bookman*, a glossy, splendidly-illustrated monthly. He was too kind for distinction as editor or critic; but as a man he had great character and, peeping out of eyes which were almost closed (I thought because he chain-smoked while typing his work), and rather huskily laughing as if his humour worked best in whispers, was good company. The Savage is now in Carlton House Terrace, full as ever of almost equally good company; more bohemian than any other London club of standing; and rich in musical and theatrical talent. Its literary interests are incidental; but it is friendly to all, including writers.

The Garrick, in Garrick Street, is full of writers, actors, and publishers. You enter a massive doorway, and are instantly among the famous theatrical portraits, which hang everywhere and make an historic collection. I should say that this club and the Savile, in Brook Street, west of Bond Street, are those in which the combination of general cordiality with proper individual reserve is best maintained. Both are associated with great figures of the past and present; both have strong literary links. The Savile was the club in which George Saintsbury, Andrew Lang, and the two Stevensons talked with high gusto.

At a later date (this was when the club was still in Piccadilly, and I was a member) I used to see G. S. Street, young in the nineties, and then apparently destined for fame as a novelist of minute comedy. He had ceased to write novels; but was an admired essayist. And he had become Examiner of Plays. Something had happened to one of his eyes, over which he wore a black patch; he drank half a pint of port after dinner every night; and, from a plump, clean, pink face, he told stories in an unmoved tone.

Today, I suppose, Compton Mackenzie and Eric Linklater have taken the place of Lang and the Stevensons; Mackenzie in particular continues in himself and his grand talent for narrative and pun and drollery every tradition of the great talkers of the past. He does not pontificate, in the Johnsonian manner; but if any man was ever a cause that wit and idleness is in other men, he is that man. The Savile is a good club. Men are happy there.

They are happy also at the Garrick, where, as I told you, Thackeray and Dickens were both members, and where so many writers since their day have found themselves at home. W. B. Maxwell, the son of Miss Braddon, was a member, a novelist who will be revived for his great qualities as soon as it occurs to somebody to extol him in form. Hugh Walpole was a member; it was at the Garrick that I first saw him. A. A. Milne, St John Ervine, and other dramatists belong; Charles Morgan is a member. Publishers are strongly represented.

They are also strongly represented at the Reform, the literary glories of which have been lessened of late years by death. James Payn, Barrie, and Henry James were old members. When I first joined, the men who gravitated naturally to one another included Wells, Bennett, Charles Masterman, Philip Gibbs, and Arthur Clutton-Brock; editors such as A. G. Gardiner, J. A. Spender, and H. W. Massingham; and scholars or professors such as John Sargeaunt, T. E. Page, and W. H. R. Rivers. Siegfried Sassoon and E. M. Forster were younger than these. All the old ones are dead; Sassoon, Forster, David Garnett, and other ornaments of the literary scene are today rare visitors. If it were not for a younger generation still, of whose talents I am confident, although I cannot identify the corporeal shells, I should have supposed the Reform to have ceased to be literary as it has ceased to be political. But it has not ceased to be literary; it is still very distinguished; and large enough and "democratic" enough to be at once aloof and friendly, as in my opinion a club should be.

Next door but one to the Reform, as you go east, is the Athenaeum. This is the most august club of all; the one at which most of the jokes at the expense of clubs by those who never enter them are levelled. On being elected to the Athenaeum men have been known in the past to drop all their other clubs; and once, when I lunched there, my host asked, as we left, where I was going. I said "The Reform," meaning, you understand, "next door but one." He said, as if the Reform dwelt on an inferior planet, "Oh, can I drop you?" But I must not suggest that there is any condescension in the Athenaeum. It is select, and it has dignity. That is its right.

4 Farewell

I have now reached the end of my account of the Bookman's London. I hope I have not lost you on the way. I have tried to tell something of what I know about authors, publishers, the streets and resting-places in which authors and publishers have been found over a great many years. London is a stupendous city; but the London of the bookman is only a part of that city. It lies between the ruins of Paternoster Row and, nowadays, the purlieus of Hampstead, Hammersmith, and, on the south side of the Thames, Dulwich. The City has largely ceased to house publishers, who are concentrated around Covent Garden or the British Museum, with old masters in Albemarle Street and delightful young ones as far west as Beauchamp Place; the immense Hutchinson group in a great building in Stratford Place; Methuens still in Essex Street, Strand; and other houses scattered here and there in all manner of strange side-streets. The trade in books has never been in a more parlous condition; costs rise, published prices are only allowed to creep in pursuit of them. Novels, I am told, which when I was a boy were nominally six shillings but in fact, owing to discounts, only four and sixpence apiece, will have to go to twelve and sixpence. And as for "serious" books, like *The Bookman's London*, their prices will mount to such a height that impoverished book-buyers will hesitate more than they ever did to stock the perishable.

I expect that books will survive as long as London survives. Book-sellers will look despairingly at their overheads; publishers will realise ever more strongly that the best-seller which eats up paper supplies is not the boon it used to be; and authors will either earn livings out-side the book trade, using literary composition as a hobby and contra-dicting what Dr Johnson said about blockheads, or they will con-centrate on Hollywood, or cultivate their gardens and go in, as Wells thought they ought to do, for plain living and high thinking on the pittance allowed them by a starved and hopeless State. I hope not to live until that age of stoicism. But, if it comes, will it be very different from earlier ages, when authors had not been spoiled by Victorian plenty? I leave you with the thought.

Index

De Quincey, Thomas, 110
Dickens, Charles, 2, 13, 33, 119 *et seq.*, 122 *et seq.*, 128, 151
Disraeli, Benjamin, 31
Dobell, Bertram, 70/1
Dodsley (publisher), 36, 38, 60
Donne, John, 15/16
Doran, George, 38, 150
Doubleday's, 62
Downey, Edmund, 40
Drinkwater, John, 150
Dryden, John, 37, 56, 76, 81, 146, 149
Duckworth's, 8
Duckworth, Gerald, 48
Du Maurier, George, 128

Edwardes, Marian, 143
Eliot, George, 120, 123–5
Ervine, St John G., 140, 154
Evans, Frederick H., 48, 68

Faber, Geoffrey, 61
Fell, Granville, 9
FitzGerald, Edward, 120 *et seq.*, 128
Fitzstephen, William, 78
Forster, E. M., 155
Forster, John, 115, 123
Fox, Caroline, 111
Fox, C. J., 99
Franklin, Benjamin, 104
Froude, J. A., 122
Fuseli, 118

Galsworthy, John, 59, 139
Gardiner, A. G., 154
Gardner, Edmund, 48
Garnett, Constance, 54
Garnett, Edward, 8, 52, 61, 140
Garrick, David, 13, 99
Garvice, Charles, 153
Gay, John, 12, 79/80
Gibbon, Edward, 99, 144, 147
Gibbs, Sir Philip, 140, 150, 154
Gissing, George, 13, 44, 132, 134/5, 149
Glaishers (booksellers), 73
Godolphin, Earl of, 82

Godwin, William, 112 *et seq.*
Goldsmith, Oliver, 77, 89, 92 *et seq.*, 105
Gollancz, Israel, 48
Gollancz, Victor, 61
Gorst, Harold, 6
Gorst, Sir John, 6
Gosse, Edmund, 42, 54, 129, 140
Graves, Clo (Dehan), 54
Gray, Thomas, 89, 91/2, 96
Griffiths, Ralph, 93

Hamilton, Hamish, 62
Hammond, Hammond, 62
Hands, Charlie, 152
Hardy, Thomas, 40, 62, 132–4
Harley, Robert, Earl of Oxford, 24, 81–3
Harrap, George, 61
Harrods bookshop, 69
Harvey, Sir J. Martin, 9
Hatchards, 68
Hawkesworth, Dr John, 101
Hawkins, Sir John, 101
Haydon, B. R., 115, 117 *et seq.*
Hazlitt, William, 12, 75, 77, 100, 109, 111, 113, 126
Heinemann, William, 8, 46, 54
Herbert, Sir A. P., 150
Herringman, Henry, 15
Hewlett, Maurice, 48, 62
Hichens, Robert, 55/6
Hobbes, John Oliver, 52
Hogarth, William, 13, 32, 97
Hollings bookshop, 73
Hotten, John Camden, 42
Housman, A. E., 57
Howard, Wren, 61
Hudson, W. H., 9, 48
Humphreys, Arthur, 68
Hunt, John, 115
Hunt, Leigh, 113 *et seq.*, 117, 119, 124, 128
Hutchinson, George, 55
Hutton, Edward, 48
Huxley, Aldous, 51, 70
Hytch of Chatto's, 70

Irving, Washington, 94
Isbisters, 8

Jacobs, W. W., 13, 27 *et seq.*
James I, 17
James, Henry, 54, 78, 134-6, 154
Jerrold, Douglas, 153
Jerrold, Walter, 153
Jewsbury, Geraldine, 122
John, Augustus, 150
Johnson, Dr, 1, 10, 35, 66, 77, 89, 94
et seq., 100 *et seq.*, 104, 143
Jones and Evans, 68
Jones, Henry Festing, 127
Jonson, Ben, 13, 16 *et seq.*, 32, 146
Joseph, Michael 62

Keats, John, 115, 116 *et seq.*
Kipling, Rudyard, 59, 62, 140

Lamb, Charles, 20, 38, 104 *et seq.*,
108 *et seq.*, 153
Lamb, Mary, 106, 112
Lamley's (booksellers), 67
Landseer, Sir E., 124
Lane, Allen, 49
Lane, John, 46, 48/9
Lang, Andrew, 154
Langton, Bennet, 99
Lawrence, D. H., 54, 60
Lee, Sir Sidney, 15
Lewes, G. H., 124/5
Linklater, Eric, 154
Lockier, Dean, 85
Longman, C. J., 45
Longman's, 36, 42
Lubbock, Sir John, 67
Lucas, E. V., 34, 57, 152
Lyall, Edna, 55
Lyons, Neil, 13

Macaulay, T. B., 76, 120, 128
Macdonald, William, 48
Mackenzie, Compton, 58, 141, 149,
154

Macmillan's, 8, 36, 42, 46
Mason, A. E. W., 140
Massingham, H. W., 154
Masterman, C. F. G., 154
Mathews, Elkin, 46
Maugham, Somerset, 54, 140, 150
Maunsell, Andrew, 36
Maxwell, W. B., 154
Melville, Herman, 126
Meredith, George, 8, 132, 134
Methuen, Sir A., 50, 55-7
Methuen's, 8
Meynell, Francis, 149
Meynell, Viola, 149
Mill, James, 75
Mills and Boon, 59
Milne, A. A., 154
Milnes, Richard Monckton, 76
Milton, John, 75
Mitford, Mary Russell, 120, 125
Moore, George, 36, 40, 42, 45, 53, 129,
131
Moore, Thomas, 112
Morgan, Charles, 53, 154
Morgan, William de, 54
Morley, John, 52, 62
Morris, William, 128, 129
Murphy, Arthur, 97, 99
Murray, John, 5, 36, 38, 42, 45, 60

Nash, Eveleigh, 58
Newbery, John, 93, 95
Newton, Sir I., 102
Nicholson, William, 54
Nollekens, Joseph, 100
Nollekens, Mrs, 115
North, Roger, 37
Northcote, James, 100, 117

Ouida, 50

Parke, Ernest, 6
Paterson, William, 52
Payn, James, 50, 134, 154
Pepys, Samuel, 12, 13, 78